Magna Carta
history, context and influence

Papers delivered at Peking University on
the 800th anniversary of Magna Carta

Edited by
Lawrence Goldman

LONDON
INSTITUTE OF HISTORICAL RESEARCH

Published by

UNIVERSITY OF LONDON
SCHOOL OF ADVANCED STUDY
INSTITUTE OF HISTORICAL RESEARCH
Senate House, Malet Street, London WC1E 7HU

2018

Available to download free at http://www.humanities-digital-library.org
or to purchase at https://www.sas.ac.uk/publications

ISBN
978 1 909646 87 2 (paperback edition)
978 1 909646 88 9 (PDF edition)

Contents

One of four known surviving 1215 exemplars of Magna Carta
(British Library Cotton MS Augustus II.106).

List of illustrations

Foreword

The papers in this collection were given at Peking University (PKU) in Beijing at a conference held on 10–11 September 2015. The event, entitled 'Retrospect and prospect: the 800th anniversary of Magna Carta' was, in fact, the third Anglo Chinese historians' conference organized between the Institute of Historical Research in London and the historians of PKU acting on behalf of historians of Britain in China in general. Our host, Professor Qian Chengdan, professor of history at PKU, had specifically requested that we hold a conference on Magna Carta and its influence, and the papers in the collection reflect the interest of Chinese scholars not only in the making of Magna Carta in 1215 but its enduring relevance in Britain, the west and now globally.

A group of eight historians went from Britain to Beijing. At the conference they were partnered by nine Chinese scholars who also gave papers. The full proceedings of the conference, the schedule of which is included in this collection, will be published in Chinese in 2018. Here, we publish the papers given by the British contingent only. Written and presented to a Chinese audience, many of whom had interests in more modern British history, these papers are necessarily broad in compass and general in approach. We were conscious that we were writing for an audience interested above all in the major themes of 1215 and the enduring qualities of Magna Carta rather than the minutiae. But this may be one of the advantages of the collection: the papers here, written for an international audience, explain and preserve the essence of Magna Carta and its meaning.

For their part, our Chinese counterparts were interested in Magna Carta's reputation and influence in China; in the meaning of 'liberty' as enshrined in the document and as interpreted by subsequent generations; in parallel developments in Chinese history which might be compared with the events in England in the early thirteenth century; and in its specifically religious and episcopal contexts. The paper delivered by Professor Gao Dai of the history department at PKU was a wonderfully entertaining, whimsical and also serious contribution linking 1215 with the present, by way of environmental history. Noting that clause 33 of Magna Carta stipulated a prohibition on weirs in the rivers Thames and Medway in order to encourage salmon, Gao Dai showed that from the seventeenth to the mid nineteenth century the clause was ignored and the salmon, overfished and unable to navigate the rivers, consequently died out. But recent improvement to the ecology of the Thames has seen the welcome return of the salmon, a small but telling connection of the present to Magna Carta's origin.

The conference was attended by faculty members from PKU, historians from many other Chinese universities, and postgraduate students. The quality of the questions and comments from the latter group assure us that the future of British historical studies in China will be very bright indeed. Discussion was always rich and engaging, but was especially lively whenever comparisons were made between social structures and legal forms in the Song, Jin and Liao eras in Chinese history and the twelfth and thirteenth centuries in England and Europe more generally. Thus we fulfilled another of the aims of these Anglo-Chinese meetings, held every three years: that we should not only learn about each other's history, but compare and contrast national developments.

Our Chinese hosts were wonderfully generous. The five-day visit included a day trip to the Great Wall as well as sightseeing in Beijing. We would like to thank Professor Qian Chengdan in particular for planning the academic programme and presiding at the conference, and Liang Yuetian of the history department at PKU for organizing our itinerary with such ease and good humour. We were assisted by many postgraduates while in Beijing and two in particular, both studying British history, deserve special thanks: Yongchun Xie of PKU and Zhang Yekai who is now at work on a Ph.D. in the history department at Brown University in the United States.

The Institute of Historical Research is grateful also to Sir Robert (Bob) Worcester, chairman of the 800 Committee, which largely planned and executed the many commemorations of Magna Carta in 2015, for the personal interest he took in the academic conference from which this book has emerged and financial support provided by the 800 Committee to get the British delegates to Beijing and back.

Lawrence Goldman, Institute of Historical Research, January 2018

Notes on contributors

SOPHIE AMBLER is lecturer in later medieval British and European history at Lancaster University. She is the author of *The Song of Simon de Montfort: the Life and Death of England's First Revolutionary* (2016); *Bishops in the Political Community of England, 1213 1270* (2017); and 'Magna Carta1 its confirmation at Simon de Montfort's parliament of 1265', published in the *English Historical Review* in 2015. She was a researcher on the Arts and Humanities Research Council's Magna Carta project in 2012–13.

DAVID CARPENTER is professor of medieval history at King's College, London. He is the author of *The Struggle for Mastery: Britain 1066–1284* (2004) in the new *Penguin History of Britain* and of *Magna Carta* (2015) in the Penguin Classics series. He was the principal investigator on the Henry III Fine Rolls project, and a co-investigator of the 2012–15 Magna Carta project, both funded by the Arts and Humanities Research Council.

HARRY T. DICKINSON taught for forty years at the University of Edinburgh, latterly as Sir Richard Lodge Professor of British History. He has published extensively on eighteenth-century British politics and is the author of *Bolingbroke* (1970); *Walpole and the Whig Supremacy* (1973); *Liberty and Property: Political Ideology in Eighteenth-Century Britain* (1977); *The Politics of the People in Eighteenth-Century Britain* (1994) and *Britain and the American Revolution* (1998).

RACHEL FOXLEY is associate professor in early modern history at the University of Reading. Her book *The Levellers: Radical Political Thought in the English Revolution* was published by Manchester University Press in 2013. Her interests focus on seventeenth-century political thought, in particular on radical and republican writing, gender and the interpretation of concepts of democracy.

GEORGE GARNETT is tutorial fellow in modern history at St Hugh's College, University of Oxford where he teaches medieval history and the history of political thought from antiquity to the seventeenth century. His recent publications include *Marsilius of Padua and 'The Truth of History'* (2006) and *Conquered England: Kingship, Succession, and Tenure 1066–1166* (2007).

LAWRENCE GOLDMAN is professor of history at the Institute of Historical Research and a senior research fellow of St. Peter's College, Oxford where he taught modern British and American history for twenty-four years. He was the editor of the *Oxford Dictionary of National Biography 2004–2014* and is the author of books on the history of worker's education; on Victorian social science; and most recently, a biography of the political thinker and historian, R. H. Tawney (2013).

ALEXANDER LOCK is a specialist in eighteenth-century British political history and curator of modern archives and manuscripts at the British Library. He co-curated the modern historical sections of the British Library's highly acclaimed exhibition *Magna Carta: Law, Liberty, Legacy* in 2015 and has published widely on issues relating to Magna Carta and public history. His book *Catholicism, Identity and Politics in the Age of Enlightenment* was published by Boydell and Brewer in 2016.

NICHOLAS VINCENT is professor of history at the University of East Anglia and a fellow of the British Academy. He has published widely on aspects of English and European history in the twelfth and thirteenth centuries including *A Brief History of Britain: The Birth of the Nation 1066–1485* (2011); *Magna Carta: a Very Short Introduction* (2012); and *Magna Carta: Making and Legacy* (2015). Between 2012 and 2015 he led the Arts and Humanities Research Council project on the historical background to Magna Carta. He is currently finishing an edition of the charters of the Plantagenet kings and queens from Henry II to King John.

第三届中英英国史学术交流研讨会

Retrospect and prospect:
800th anniversary of Magna Carta

Papers delivered by Chinese scholars
at the Magna Carta conference

1. Historic anniversaries in British public life: Magna Carta 800/2015 in perspective

Lawrence Goldman

The 800th anniversary celebrations of Magna Carta offer an opportunity to judge not only the importance of the document and the influence of its ideas on Britons today, but to consider also the growing British fascination with historical anniversaries of all sorts. In recent years a distinctive feature of British public life has been the number of historic anniversaries we not only register but mark in some public way, whether through celebrations or ceremonies of a more sombre type. Many of these are connected with the two twentieth-century world wars which have defined British identity and shaped British history like nothing else has in the modern period. Whether the commemoration of the 70th anniversary of the D-Day landings in June 2014, the centenary of the outbreak of the First World War two months later, or the Battles of Agincourt (1415) and Waterloo (1815) as well as the 800th anniversary of the sealing of Magna Carta in 2015, the British have become addicted to historical anniversaries, many of them military in nature. Each new year begins with the publication of the lists of historic anniversaries to follow over the next twelve months.[1] If we awaken early enough each morning, at 5.35am on BBC Radio 4 great and notable events which occurred on this day in history are listed and sometimes explained, as if to encourage us out of bed to do something notable in the day to come as our forebears did notable things before us.[2] It is reminiscent of the St. Crispin's Day speech in *Henry V*:

> And gentlemen in England now a-bed
> Shall think themselves accurs'd they were not here[3]

---

[1] See, for example, the 2016 list on the Visit England website: <https://www.visitengland.com/biz/advice-and-support/travel-trade/anniversaries-2016>. This includes reference not only to the 400th anniversary of Shakespeare's death and the 300th anniversary of the birth of Capability Brown, but the centenary of Roald Dahl's birth and the 950th anniversary of the battle of Hastings.

[2] For a comprehensive list of anniversaries relevant internationally, see <https://en.wikipedia.org/wiki/List_of_historical_anniversaries>.

[3] Shakespeare, *Henry V*, IV. iii.

L. Goldman, 'Historic anniversaries in British public life: Magna Carta 800/2015 in perspective', in *Magna Carta: history, context and influence*, ed. L. Goldman (2018), pp. 1–15.

1

There is even an 'On This Day' BBC website listing daily events in the period 1950–2005, effectively covering the television age before the advent of the internet age.[4]

The British have always been a historically minded people who have used history for contemporary political and civic purposes. But the recent desire to acknowledge our past in so many ways and so many places is worthy of some consideration, especially in the light of the public activities and projects connected with Magna Carta across Britain in 2015. What does the remembrance of Magna Carta tell us about the status of anniversaries in British public life and national consciousness, and how should historians think about the growing propensity to remember British – and other – history in this manner?

The 2015 celebrations for Magna Carta came to a climax at Runnymede, in the meadow where the document was sealed on 15 June 1215 800 years previously, in the presence of the Queen and Prince William, the archbishop of Canterbury and the prime minister, David Cameron.[5] The audience had assembled there early on a damp and faintly misty June morning, though they were soon exceedingly hot with no shade under a strong sun. There were speeches; bands and orchestras played; choirs sang; people chatted amiably and the atmosphere was more village fête – though for an event for 3,500 people – than political event or historical commemoration.[6] Fittingly, the morning's activities ended with a flypast by the Red Arrows, the RAF's elite aerial acrobatics team, who grace many a British festival. Probably the largest cheer of the morning was given before the speech of the United States' attorney general, Loretta Lynch, representing the U.S. government and people.[7] But this was not in virtue of the Anglo-American 'special relationship', or the American veneration of Magna Carta, which is palpably greater than in Britain. Rather, it was for her role in the arrest and detention

---

[4] <http://news.bbc.co.uk/onthisday/default.stm>.

[5] 'Magna Carta changes the world, David Cameron tells anniversary event' <http://www.bbc.co.uk/news/uk-33126723>; 'Magna Carta: leaders celebrate 800th anniversary of the Great Charter', *The Guardian*, 15 June 2015 <http://www.theguardian.com/uk-news/2015/jun/15/magna-carta-leaders-celebrate-800th-anniversary-runnymede>; 'Authors of Magna Carta would be "bemused" by celebration 800 years on', *The Daily Telegraph*, 15 June 2015 <http://www.telegraph.co.uk/news/uknews/11675736/Authors-of-Magna-Carta-would-be-bemused-by-celebration-800-years-on.html>.

[6] *Magna Carta. Foundation of Liberty. Runnymede 800. 15 June 2015* (official programme, National Trust, 2015).

[7] 'British picnic on the grass and raise a pint to Magna Carta', *Washington Post*, 15 June 2015 <https://www.washingtonpost.com/world/british-gather-to-commemorate-800th-anniversary-of-magna-carta/2015/06/15/63e90a58-133d-11e5-89f3-61410da94eb1_story.html?tid=ptv_rellink>

Figure 1.1. 'The Jurors' by Huw Lock at Runnymede, Surrey, commissioned
by Surrey County Council and the National Trust to commemorate the
800th anniversary of Magna Carta in 2015. The twelve chairs represent
the historical and ongoing struggle for justice and equal rights.

in the previous days of allegedly corrupt officials from the governing body
of world football, FIFA. In a country not famed for its devotion to soccer,
the American authorities had done what no government in Europe had
dared to do despite all the evidence of misappropriation and malfeasance
by FIFA officials. Magna Carta had secured the rights of the innocent and
mandated due process under the law: many clapped and cheered Lynch for
ensuring that the rule of law would extend to the administration of 'the
beautiful game' across the world.[8]

Participants at Runnymede that morning were also able to admire
the new sculpture in the meadow by Hew Locke.[9] Called 'The Jurors', it
celebrates the famous 39th clause of Magna Carta mandating for all men
'the lawful judgment of his equals'. Locke's bronze installation takes the

[8] 'FIFA President Sepp Blatter's real foe was US Attorney General not ethics inquiry', *The
Guardian*, 21 Dec. 2015 <http://www.theguardian.com/us-news/2015/dec/21/fifa-president-
sepp-blatter-nemesis-loretta-lynch-football-new-york>.

[9] 'Sculpture at Runnymede celebrates Magna Carta's blow against injustice', *The
Guardian*, 15 June 2015 <http://www.theguardian.com/culture/2015/jun/15/hew-locke-
sculpture-jurors-runnymede-magna-carta-against-injustice>; <http://artatrunnymede.com>;
<https://photosynth.net/preview/view/71e2a982-5079-41de-ac9e-75c1d422e9d8>.

Figure 1.2. The American Bar Association Memorial to
Magna Carta at Runnymede, erected in 1957.

form of twelve chairs for twelve jury members and pays tribute not only to Magna Carta's English origins and influence in Britain but, in chairs devoted to the abolition of slavery, the emancipation of the serfs and the struggle for the freedom of Nelson Mandela, among other themes, to its influence around the world. Mandela, of course, cited the rights granted by Magna Carta in his great speech at the Rivonia trial in South Africa in 1964.[10] 'The Jurors' is a less dramatic memorial than the column that nineteenth-century satirist Richard Brinsley Sheridan proposed to erect in the meadow for the centenary of the Glorious Revolution of 1688 on 'a spot sacred to the liberties of the people'.[11] But this was never built. The celebrations planned for 1715 were never held in a tense year in British history when the new Hanoverian regime of George I was threatened with Jacobite rebellion. Nor did the planned commemorations of 1815 and 1915 take place in years in which Britain was engaged in two great wars in France and the Low Countries.

This climax to the events of 2015 was, in fact, a very British style of anticlimax, understated and casual rather than scripted and formal. This was in keeping with the planning and organization of the Magna Carta anniversary from the first which had fallen to the '800 Committee' under the aegis of the Magna Carta Trust which had been formed in 1956.[12] The 800 Committee included public figures, politicians, jurists, academics and representatives of those institutions which hold copies of Magna Carta, among them cathedrals and great libraries.[13] But until the grant of £1 million by the chancellor of the exchequer, George Osborne, in his 2014 Budget speech – and this can hardly be considered magnificent public largesse – the 800 Committee and the preparation of the Magna Carta memorials entrusted to it had been largely supported by an individual, Sir Robert (Bob) Worcester, an American domiciled in England and famous for his long career in British political polling, who chaired the 800 Committee. Until 2012 most of the available public funds for cultural activity went to support the London Olympics; only latterly did the state recognize the significance of 2015, and, interestingly, having made a grant to the Magna Carta commemorations, central funds were then found, on the same model,

---

[10] <http://artatrunnymede.com/magna-carta-nelson-mandela/>; <http://www.bl.uk/magna-carta/articles/magna-carta-in-the-modern-age>.

[11] *Annual Register*, 1788, pp. 220, 249–51, cited in R. Quinault, 'The cult of the centenary, c.1784–1914', . *Research*, lxxi (1998), 303–23, at p. 305.

[12] <http://magnacarta800th.com>.

[13] <http://magnacarta800th.com/magna-carta-today/membership-of-the-magna-carta-800th-committee/>.

for the commemorations of Agincourt and Waterloo in 2015 as well.[14] The British and Commonwealth campaign at Gallipoli in 1915, one of the many disastrous campaigns of the First World War, was not forgotten, either. On 25 April 2015, ANZAC Day, there were ceremonies at the Australian and New Zealand War Memorials in Hyde Park and at the Cenotaph in Whitehall, London. On the previous day, there had been a commemorative service at the Cape Hellas memorial at Gallipoli itself. Each of these was attended by members of the British royal family.[15]

None of these military anniversaries evoked the crescendo of interest that attached to Magna Carta in 2015. The interest was all the more effective as a tool of public education because it was largely generated from below by academic, church, community and local groups given small sums for their projects, exhibitions and celebrations.[16] In a very British fashion, the energy and interest was self-generated rather than imposed or choreographed from above. There were notable exhibitions, such as that in Westminster Hall which brought the four surviving original Magna Cartas to a single place, and the British Library exhibition 'Law, Liberty and Legacy' which ran for much of the year, designed by Dr Claire Breay, lead curator of medieval and early manuscripts at the British Library.[17] Among several academic conferences, that held in June at King's College London and the British Library was the most notable in bringing together all the leading historians.[18] Magna Carta featured on several major websites including those of The National Archives,[19] the Historical Association,[20] Salisbury Cathedral[21] and many smaller and less well-known ones. There were church services and thanksgivings; commemorative coins and postage stamps; local exhibitions and lectures; books and learned articles; school lessons aplenty; and several major television and radio programmes, such as the series devoted to Magna Carta's history and legacy in BBC Radio 4's 'In Our Time' strand.[22] The celebrations and commemorations were not without a

---

[14] <http://www.agincourt600.com>; <http://waterloo200.org/about/>.

[15] Royal British Legion: Gallipoli Centenary: <http://www.britishlegion.org.uk/ remembrance/what-we-remember/gallipolicentenary/?gclid=CjoKEQiA6IC2BRDcjPrjm_ istoUBEiQASrLz1k1rR_uonafbX7WJorDnky62eVomBYD9V5NEvesURwUaAj_ t8P8HAQ>.

[16] <http://magnacarta800th.com/projects/>

[17] <http://www.bl.uk/events/magna-carta--law-liberty-legacy>; *Magna Carta: Law, Liberty, Legacy*, ed. C. Breay and J. Harrison (2015).

[18] <http://magnacarta.cmp.uea.ac.uk/read/conference>.

[19] <http://www.nationalarchives.gov.uk/education/medieval/magna-carta/>.

[20] <https://www.history.org.uk/news/news_2510.html>.

[21] <http://www.salisburycathedral.org.uk/magna-carta>.

[22] <http://www.bbc.co.uk/programmes/book4fg7>.

scholarly purpose and outcome as well. Thanks to a large grant in 2012 from the Arts and Humanities Research Council to Professor Nicholas Vincent at the University of East Anglia for a three-year project to track down lost originals of Magna Carta and create an online database about the document and its textual and manuscript history, two new copies were found.[23] Both were Magna Cartas dating from 1300 and both were originally from Kent. One was from Faversham and the other, found in the Kent County Archives along with the town's Charter of the Forest, had originally been in the possession of the town of Sandwich.[24]

Inevitably among such a range of commemorations, the import of Magna Carta became blurred, distorted and anachronistic. It was celebrated too often as a cornerstone of modern 'democracy' in some generalized way, rather than the rule of law, the rights of the subject, and due legal process.[25] Nevertheless, there can be little doubt that all this activity had its effect: the sheer number of local projects and commemorations is testimony to the interest people took in the anniversary and its penetration into the collective 'national mind', if only for a few weeks in mid 2015. The Magna Carta anniversary celebrations may be the best evidence of British historical consciousness today, but they are hardly the only example of the marking and observance of anniversaries in our public life. Indeed, their prominence and success in 2015 owed a great deal to a public culture which has been highly interested and engaged in historical remembrance since at least the 1980s.

For academic historians the significance of modern public anniversaries can be best approached via the emergence of two relatively recent sub-disciplines: the history of memory and the history of traditions. Eric Hobsbawm related the 'invention of traditions' to the development of modern nations and states in the nineteenth century and their requirement for a shared history and ceremonies by which to create national cohesion. Previous forms of solidarity had been based on religion, duty to a sovereign, regional or even tribal association. The new nation states in Europe and the Americas had to replace these with a national narrative which could be

[23] <https://www.uea.ac.uk/about/media-room/press-release-archive/-/asset_publisher/a2jEGMiFHPhv/content/university-of-east-anglia-unveils-magna-carta-research-project>; <http://magnacartaresearch.org>.

[24] 'Magna Carta edition found in Sandwich archive scrapbook', *BBC News*, 8 Feb. 2015 <http://www.bbc.co.uk/news/uk-england-31242433>; 'Faversham: Magna Carta rediscovered' <http://magnacarta800th.com/projects/round-1-grants/faversham-magna-carta-rediscovered/>.

[25] 'In this field of dreams, democracy was born', *Daily Telegraph*, 16 June 2015.

dramatized through anniversary.[26] Hence the first celebrations of Bastille Day, 14 July, waited until 1880 and came at a time when the French Third Republic was struggling to legitimize republicanism, unify a nation, and turn 'peasants into Frenchmen'.[27] Roland Quinault's work on the history of public anniversaries, specifically centenaries, adds detail and texture to this broad thesis. Their observance emerged later than might be expected in the last third of the nineteenth century. Unlike twentieth-century observance, centenaries then tended to celebrate writers and cultural figures rather than military heroes and military events. The British state was not greatly involved: they were the work of enthusiasts and followers. The development of mass transportation and the growth of leisure assisted public participation. If they encouraged national solidarity, centenaries and anniversaries were made possible by the emergence of a mature historical consciousness in the final decades of the nineteenth century.[28] The rise in historical interest and publication in these years, the development of major public institutions like the National Portrait Gallery which gave popular access to Britain's past, the introduction of history as a degree course in universities and its institutionalization in the school curriculum, and the systematic gathering and cataloguing of historical documents in major collections, raised public awareness of the past and made the public anniversary possible.

Some of the most notable anniversaries still celebrated in Britain were spontaneous acts of memorialization, emerging from the natural desire of populations to remember events and bear witness to the changes to their lives. Armistice Day, 11 November, emerged in this manner directly after the First World War, part spontaneous, part planned, and rapidly won pride of place in the British public's annual ceremonial traditions.[29] Indeed, it supplanted the annual celebration of the Battle of Trafalgar of 21 October 1805, which throughout the nineteenth century had been a major anniversary both in Britain and across the empire.[30] After the First World War it was felt to be inappropriate to mark military victory in this manner and public mourning and remembrance took the place of celebration. Guy Fawkes Day, 5 November, also emerged rapidly after the events of 1605 in which Roman Catholic plotters were caught before they were able

---

[26] E. Hobsbawm, 'Mass-producing traditions: Europe, 1870–1914' in *The Invention of Tradition*, ed. E. Hobsbawm and T. Ranger (Cambridge, 1983; rev. edn. 1992), pp. 263–307.

[27] Hobsbawm, 'Mass-producing traditions', p. 271. See E. Weber, *Peasants into Frenchmen: the Modernization of Rural France 1870–1914* (Stanford, Calif., 1976).

[28] Quinault, 'The cult of the centenary', pp. 320–3.

[29] A. Gregory, *The Silence of Memory: Armistice Day 1919–1946* (Providence, R.I., 1994).

[30] W. Shephard Walsh, *Curiosities of Popular Customs and Rites, Ceremonies, Observances and Miscellaneous Antiquities* (1898), p. 940.

to blow up parliament: almost immediately 'national deliverance' was celebrated widely across England and remembrance was institutionalized by the passage of the Observance of 5th November Act, widely known as the 'Thanksgiving Act', in January 1606, which mandated celebration and prayer on 5 November each year in thanks for the salvation of the king and legislators. The anniversary became a ritualized means for the denunciation and persecution of Roman Catholics; later, in the 1630s and 1640s, it was used by puritans as an occasion to denounce their political and religious enemies, royalists and all alleged crypto-Catholics.[31]

The Magna Carta commemorations in 2015 led to nothing like this. The events of 1215 are too far in the past to create conflict as opposed to curiosity. The principles that Magna Carta embodied and has represented ever since are too central and precious to British and western political values and judicial systems to evoke dissent. There has been academic debate, as there should be: for example, the argument of the senior judge of the Supreme Court, Jonathan Sumption, who is also a leading medieval historian, that Magna Carta's importance has been exaggerated, was controversial.[32] There was criticism of David Cameron for using his speech at the ceremony at Runnymede on 15 June to exalt a putative British Bill of Rights of the future above the Human Rights Act of the present, passed by the Labour government in 1998 and disliked by many Conservatives because of its perceived bias in favour of individual petitioners.[33] Cameron told the gathering that 'here in Britain, ironically the place where those ideas were first set out, the good name of human rights has sometimes become distorted and devalued'. The mixing of party politics with national commemoration was not well received. In Beijing, an exhibition of the Hereford Cathedral Magna Carta at Renmin University was cancelled and relocated to the British embassy when the necessary ministerial approvals were not forthcoming.[34] But these were relatively insignificant controversies and conflicts when set against the wider history of anniversaries and their celebration in British history.

The very success of the Magna Carta celebrations and the interest in

[31] J. A. Sharpe, *Remember, Remember: a Cultural History of Guy Fawkes Day* (Cambridge, Mass., 2005); D. Cressy, 'The fifth of November remembered', in *Myths of the English*, ed. R. Porter (1992).

[32] J. Sumption, 'Magna Carta then and now', address to the Friends of the British Library, 9 March 2015 <https://www.supremecourt.uk/docs/speech-150309.pdf>.

[33] 'David Cameron: I'll fix human rights mess', *BBC News*, 15 June 2015 <http://www.bbc.co.uk/news/uk-politics-33134338>.

[34] 'Magna Carta not welcome at Beijing University' <http://magnacarta800th.com/articles/magna-carta-not-welcome-at-beijing-university/>.

anniversaries raise questions about a society so much given to retrospection: it may reinforce the view that Britain is a society with a better past than future and is fixated on lost glory.[35] On the other hand, it may also be evidence of the remarkable success of history as a discipline in Britain today. On television and radio, in newspapers and magazines, on bookshelves and in libraries, history is popular and finds a ready audience – and this audience can appreciate the celebration of the past and participate fully in it. Certainly the commemoration of national anniversaries provides us with a type of national cohesion, though this may in itself simply be a replacement for other types of solidarity. Most religious ritual, ceremony and festivity is an act of remembrance – be it the birth and death of Jesus at Christmas and Easter; or the deliverance of the children of Israel from Egyptian slavery at Passover.

Some anniversaries are untroubled and untroubling, notably those commemorating events from the distant past or those that remember sacrifice in a self-evidently virtuous struggle such as the defeat of Nazism in the Second World War. But remembering the First World War is more difficult because the cause Britain fought for does not seem so just and noble now, and because the First World War is seen to have been badly managed by politicians and generals who, in the popular view of the war, needlessly sacrificed hundreds of thousands of British lives. The remembrance of national heroes is also easily accomplished. Winston Churchill's reputation has only grown since his death in 1965, ensuring that the fiftieth anniversary in January 2015 was quite without criticism. In the 1960s and 1970s his mistakes were more prominent in public discussion, and it was common to hear and read reference to Tonypandy in 1911 (where as home secretary Churchill used troops to shut down a strike of Welsh coal miners); Gallipoli in 1915 (which was Churchill's idea); going back onto the gold standard at the pre-war exchange rate in 1925 when he was chancellor of the exchequer; and his support for King Edward VIII in 1936 during the abdication crisis. Sometimes, an anniversary can usefully encapsulate a movement or an idea. A recent conference at the Institute of Historical Research in London on the relationship between science and modernism in the period 1880–1920 exactly coincided with the centenary of the first ever use of poison gas in warfare on 22 April 1915 in France on the Western Front.[36] What better way to point to the ambiguities in the history of technology and of 'progress' itself than to remind the audience of this dark centenary?

---

[35] P. Wright, *On Living in an Old Country: the National Past in Contemporary Britain* (1985)

[36] 'Being modern: science and culture in the early twentieth century', 22–4 Apr. 2015, IHR, London <http://www.history.ac.uk/events/browse/17866>.

Few anniversaries are without their attendant moral and national difficulties. Remembering the Second World War will be different for other combatant societies – for Germany and Japan, of course, and also for Russia and China, where the scale of what occurred and what is to be remembered is so different from British historical experience. There have been various arguments and disagreements over Second World War anniversaries: arguments over who sacrificed more; over who liberated the French (almost always the Americans); over the presence of German representatives at ceremonial events; and of the omission of due acknowledgment at the D-Day commemorations in 2014 of the role of Canadian personnel on 6 June 1944. The bombing of Dresden in February 1945 reignites controversy in Britain each year. To some Britons, the fact that the nation defines itself through the remembrance of conflicts and warfare is no sort of recommendation, and they object to the 'militarization of remembrance'. In early November each year, most Britons wear a poppy in the lapel of their jackets and coats. It is timed to coincide with the anniversary of 11 November 1918, the day the First World War ended. The poppy we wear is a plastic flower, red in colour, to remind us of the real red poppies which grew on the battlefields of Flanders between 1914 and 1918: it is a national symbol of remembrance, perhaps the most notable of all personal, British symbols. But some critics today wear *white* poppies instead, distributed by the Peace Pledge Union which was founded in 1934, because they object to symbols of conflict and violence and to the glorification of warfare as they see it.[37]

The same event can therefore be remembered and experienced in different ways. This was made clear to me on 9 May 1990 when leading a party of students to Moscow under the old Soviet Union. We encountered a group of men wearing British military decorations, members of the North Russia Club which united comrades who had served at the Royal Navy bases in Archangel and Murmansk in northern Russia during the Second World War. Membership was later extended to all those who had served on the Arctic convoys to Russia supplying the Soviet Union with war materiel – guns, ammunition, supplies – from 1941.[38] Their role in the war had been largely forgotten in Britain, and commemorating our alliance with Stalin was difficult during the Cold War. But these men came every year to Soviet commemorations of the end of the war and they looked on the Russians as their comrades and friends.

[37] <http://www.ppu.org.uk/whitepoppy/>.
[38] The North Russia Club was wound up in 2007. There is still an Arctic Convoy Club. See <https://www.google.co.uk/search?q=arctic+convoy+club&sa=X&biw=1280&bih=907& tbm=isch&tbo=u&source=univ&ved=0ahUKEwiLyJSTkv_KAhUBVxQKHWiK CqUQsAQIVQ>

There are many anniversaries in the British calendar that are intrinsically controversial. The annual Guy Fawkes celebrations were occasions for the stigmatization of Roman Catholics, as we have seen. In 2014 many British television programmes and articles conveyed a message that the First World War was purposeless, meaningless carnage. Yet to many of the men who marched away to fight, the war had a powerful rationale in stopping 'Prussianism' and the domination of great powers over smaller nations seeking to be free. To them it was a fight for international order and liberalism, though this commitment has largely been overlooked in subsequent literary, dramatic and musical explorations of the war. Hiroshima Day, 6 August, has been taken up not only by peace movements in general, but by those who would distort the history of the use of atomic weapons and present it as a crime, rather than present it in its own unique historical context. Controversy attends any historical commemoration where the issues remain unresolved – for example, the centenary of the American Civil War in the early 1960s at a time when the same issues of African-American civil rights were still being fought over in the United States.[39] It was difficult to avoid controversy and many American organizations, whether official or private, gave up the attempt at remembrance, or did so in a carefully muted fashion. Only military remembrance was possible on the basis of the shared heroism and sacrifice of both sets of combatants who in the 1860s fought nobly although for different causes. But as soon as those causes came under scrutiny, remembrance was pitched into the present and became politicized rather than historicized. This was also the fate of the centenary of the Russian Revolution in 2017. It was impossible to note the anniversary of the Bolshevik coup without noting also the crimes of the Soviet Union, its disregard for human life and truth, its inauspicious collapse, but the continuation of its anti-democratic and anti-western culture nonetheless. The different commemorations of 1917 were influenced not only by ideology but also by the knowledge that the Revolution, whatever the hopes for it at the time, ended in persecutions, purges, the gulags and collapse.

The annual commemoration of the Apprentice Boys of Derry/Londonderry, Northern Ireland, is in a league of its own when it comes to controversy and communal tension, even though the events recalled occurred as long ago as December 1688 when thirteen Protestant apprentice boys in Derry shut the city gates against a force of 1,200 Catholic troops.

---

[39] R. Cook, 'Ordeal of the union: Allan Nevins, the Civil War centennial and the civil rights struggle of the 1960s' in *Reconfiguring the Union: Civil War Transformations*, ed. I. Morgan and P. Davies (2013), pp. 181–200; J. Sexton, 'Projecting Lincoln, projecting America' in *The Global Lincoln*, ed. R. Carwardine and J. Sexton (Oxford, 2011), pp. 288–302.

There followed more than seven months of siege, much of it under the command of the deposed king, James II, during which it was reported that 4,000 of the townspeople, about half the population, died of starvation. The siege was eventually lifted by the forces of the new Protestant British monarch, William III, and the besieging Catholic army retreated. These events are marked each year by the ceremonial closing of the gates in December and then the biggest and most antagonistic of Northern Ireland's Orange Order parades on the second Saturday of August to remember the relief of Derry/Londonderry. Protestant parades are more than merely acts of remembrance; in tense, religiously divided communities they have been understood as acts of intimidation on the part of the majority Protestant community against the minority Catholic community in Ulster. The problem is all the more intense in Derry/Londonderry because here the nationalist community – Catholic – is actually larger than the loyalist – Protestant – population. The routes taken by the parades and marches, which are held across the cities and towns of the province, have led them by design into many Catholic districts in order to reinforce the sense of subordination felt by many Catholics. They were always controversial but became the cause of outright violence between the communities in the years of the Troubles after 1968. Policing them drew the civil and military authorities into the local conflicts as well. After particularly intense conflict over Orange Order parades in Portadown in the mid and late 1990s, an investigative commission was established to recommend ways of reducing communal friction, and under the terms of the 1998 Public Processions (Northern Ireland) Act, a permanent Parades Commission, a quasi-judicial public body, now oversees arrangements which allow Protestants to march, but in less contentious places, and Catholics to live in peace.[40] The parades – and the annual summer marching season in Northern Ireland in general – are an example of the commemoration of events which are still integral to contemporary politics. In Northern Ireland, the way history is remembered, recorded and celebrated has itself become part of the ongoing conflict between groups.

Some anniversaries, meanwhile, remember or commemorate the wrong thing. Anyone with even a passing knowledge of the French Revolution will appreciate the inflated significance that 14 July gives to the fall of the Bastille. The Bastille was a hated symbol of the corruption of the French *ancien regime*, but when the crowd overwhelmed it there were only a handful of prisoners to be released. Because it was a building that could be taken, as in a battle, it had an immediate significance. Yet, to a historian, there

---

[40] <http://www.paradescommission.org>

are far more important events in that same season, such as the pledge of 17 June 1789, taken by members of the Third Estate and the liberal nobility, to create an enduring popular assembly – or the famous debates and decisions of that assembly on 4 August 1789 to end all feudal dues and relationships, all the privileges and legal immunities of an aristocracy that had prospered at the expense of the people. The commemoration of 14 July each year may be said to hamper a true understanding of the French Revolution as a sequence of events and developments stretching across more than a decade from 1786 to the rise of Napoleon in the mid 1790s.

There are also forgotten anniversaries, those overlooked or otherwise uncelebrated. The *Oxford Dictionary of National Biography* devoted lavish resource and time to an update in October 2008 designed to coincide with the ninetieth anniversary of the end of the First World War which added several dozen biographies of people connected with the war who were missing from the Dictionary. But the update coincided with the global financial crash of that month, when the world economic system seemed on the brink of collapse, and no one took any notice.

We should also register the capacity of a public ceremonial or commemoration to transform and overshadow private remembrance such that personal responses are overwhelmed by wider, societal reactions. It is to the credit of British society that Holocaust Memorial Day on 27 January each year – the day that Auschwitz was liberated in 1945 – has been officially observed since 2001.[41] The anniversary has grown in stature and significance in recent years, so that on 27 January 2015 the prime minister, the deputy prime minister and the leader of the opposition, among others, were all engaged in a televised public act of remembrance.[42] No one could be against the efforts made thereby to ensure that this particular horror is not forgotten and that as a society, we educate the next generation about the degree of man's inhumanity to man. But grief is largely private and is not always easily shared. Public ceremonial may educate others, those who perhaps need to be educated, but can feel like an invasion to those who themselves suffered or lost family members, or have been deprived of family members never born. When we mark anniversaries of such grave events in this public manner we should be aware also of the private reactions of those affected for whom public ceremonial may feel like an invasion of the privacy and solitude that personal remembrance sometimes requires. For this reason the most potent anniversaries in the calendar are not national anniversaries

---

[41] <http://hmd.org.uk/page/about-hmdt>.

[42] <http://hmd.org.uk/news/holocaust-memorial-day-2015-uk-ceremony-honours-survivor-memory>.

of the sort investigated by historians, but personal ones, a set of individual memories that we carry with us and which pattern our lives. We recall – just about – when and where we first met our partner, when and where we learnt we were to become a mother or father, when and where we learnt of a death – and it could be the death of John F. Kennedy on 23 November 1963, which so many people then alive, all over the world, seemed to recall in the years that followed.[43]

Anniversaries structure our lives. They remind us who we are, which tribe we belong to, what we believe in and how we should understand the past. They bind us together, whether in a nation, sect or group. They can also divide us from others. But what made the 800th anniversary of Magna Carta notable was its universality based on the central ideas contained within the document itself.[44] There was much understandable public interest in the history of the early thirteenth century which brought the parties – king, bishops and nobles – to Runnymede in June 1215. There was legitimate pride in Magna Carta as a product of English history and values. But the anniversary celebrations were notable for the focus on the ideas of due process, fair and open procedures, the rule of law and the submission of all – even monarchs – to that law. This made it possible to widen the participants in, and audience for, the 800th anniversary because these ideas have an international – indeed a universal – impact far beyond the confines of England, Britain and the Commonwealth. Most anniversaries are confined by the history of the events and the biography of the individual being celebrated. Exceptionally, in 2015, the Magna Carta anniversary exceeded the boundaries of time and place and was marked and celebrated around the world, in Beijing as well as in Runnymede.

---

[43] <http://news.bbc.co.uk/onthisday/hi/dates/stories/november/22/newsid_2451000/2451143.stm>.

[44] N. Vincent, *Magna Carta: Origins and Legacy* (Oxford, 2015), p. 150.

2. Magna Carta 1215: its social and political context

David Carpenter

The year 2015 was the 800th anniversary of Magna Carta. It was on 15 June 1215 that King John, in the meadow of Runnymede beside the Thames between Windsor and Staines, authorized the writing out and sealing of the document which was to become known as Magna Carta. Runnymede remains an atmospheric place and it is not difficult to imagine the scene during those tense days in June 1215 when the Charter was being negotiated; the great pavilion of the king, like some circus top, towering over the smaller tents of barons and knights stretching out across the meadow.[1] Today the great jets taking off from London Heathrow airport come up over Runnymede and then turn to fly down its whole length before vanishing into the distance. It is as though they are taking Magna Carta round the world, and the Charter has indeed become one of the most famous documents in world constitutional history.

Magna Carta is 3,550 words long written in Latin, the English translation of the Latin Magna Carta being Great Charter. Much of the Charter, even in a modern translation, can seem remote and archaic. It abounds in terms like wainage, amercement, socage and distraint.[2] Some of its chapters seem of minor importance. One calls for the removal of fish weirs from the rivers Thames and Medway. Yet there are other chapters which still have a very clear contemporary relevance. Under chapter 12, the king is not to levy taxation without the common consent of the kingdom. Under chapter 39, he cannot arrest people or seize their property without judgement of their peers or by the law of the land. Under chapter 40, he is not to deny, delay or sell justice.[3] In these ways, the Charter asserted a fundamental principle:

---

[1] The best contemporary description of the scene is in *Radulphi de Coggeshal Chronicon Anglicanum*, ed. J. Stevenson (Rolls Ser., 1875), p. 172. The chronicler Matthew Paris explained that 'Runnymede', an English word, meant 'the meadow of counsel'. It was 'a place where from ancient times meetings had taken place about the peace of the kingdom' (*Matthaei Parisiensis Historia Anglorum*, ed. F. Madden (3 vols., Rolls Ser., 1866–9), ii. 153).

[2] D. Carpenter, *Magna Carta* (Harmondsworth, 2015), pp. 461–70 has a glossary explaining the meaning of these and other contemporary terms. The classic work on the Charter remains J.C. Holt, *Magna Carta* (2nd edn., Cambridge, 1992).

[3] Detailed commentaries on the chapters in the 1215 Magna Carta by Henry Summerson

D. Carpenter, 'Magna Carta 1215: its social and political context', in *Magna Carta: history, context and influence*, ed. L. Goldman (2018), pp. 17–24.

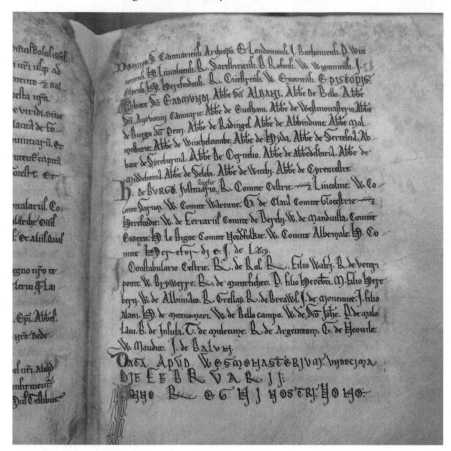

Figure 2.1. The last part of the copy of Magna Carta 1225 in the Cerne Abbey cartulary (Cambridge University Library Ll.1.10). 1225 was the first time Magna Carta was given a full witness list and the scribe at Cerne clearly recognised its importance in testifying to the way that Charter was now accepted by the good and great of the land. Photograph: David Carpenter.

that of the rule of law. The king was beneath the law, the law the Charter itself was making. He could no longer treat his subjects in an arbitrary fashion. Chapters of Magna Carta are still on the statute book of the United Kingdom today.[4] It still features in current political debate. The heading

---

may be found on the website of the Magna Carta project <http://www.magnacartaresearch. org> [accessed 22 March 2018].

  [4] For the surviving chapters and the repeal of others, see 'Magna Carta repeals': <http:// www.legislation.gov.uk/aep/Edw1cc1929/25/9/contents> [accessed 22 March 2018].

of a leader in *The Guardian* newspaper opposing the ninety-day detention period for suspected terrorists was 'Protecting Magna Carta'.[5] In 2015 chapter 40, promising that justice should not be sold, was cited by those opposing the government's changes to legal aid.

In 1215 there was nothing new in the ideas behind the Charter. They were centuries old and part of general European heritage.[6] Strengthened in the twelfth century by the study of Roman and canon law, they can be found in legislation and constitutions promulgated in Spain, Hungary and the south of France.[7] It was in England, however, that they led to the most radical and detailed restrictions on the ruler. That was because in England the ruler was uniquely demanding and intrusive, thanks to the pressures of maintaining a continental empire which stretched from Normandy to the Pyrenees. By the time of John's accession in 1199, there was already outcry at the level of the king's financial demands. They were to become far worse. After John had lost Normandy and Anjou to the king of France in 1204, he spent ten years in England amassing the cash needed to recover his empire, in the process tripling his revenues.[8] In 1214 the eventual campaign of recovery ended in total failure. John returned to England, his money spent, his prestige in tatters. The next year his baronial enemies rebelled and forced him to concede Magna Carta. They had other grievances. Although paying lip service to the principles of custom and consent, John's rule had been lawless. He took hostages at will, deprived barons of lands and castles without legal process, and demanded large sums of money to assuage his rancour and recover his good will. In a chivalrous age, which expected noble captives to be treated with courtesy, he was cruel. He murdered both his nephew Arthur and the most famous noble woman of the age, Matilda de Briouze. She and her eldest son were starved to death in the dungeons

---

[5] *The Guardian*, 5 No. 2015 <http://www.theguardian.com/politics/2005/nov/05/terrorism.terrorism> [accessed 22 March 2018]. The later history of the Charter and its influence especially in America is splendidly illustrated in N. Vincent, *Magna Carta: Origins and Legacy* (Oxford, 2015).

[6] For very similar ideas being expressed in the Carolingian period, see J. L. Nelson, 'Bad kingship in the earlier middle ages', *Haskins Soc. Jo.*, viii (1999), 1–26.

[7] See, e.g., R. Altamira, 'Magna Carta and Spanish medieval jurisprudence', in *Magna Carta Commemoration Essays*, ed. H. E. Malden (1917), pp. 227–43; T. N. Bisson, 'An "Unknown Charter" for Catalonia (A.D. 1205)', in his *Medieval France and her Neighbours* (1989), pp. 199–212; N. Vincent, 'English liberties, Magna Carta (1215) and the Spanish connection', in *1212–1214: El trienio que hizo a Europa*, Acta de la XXXVII Semana de Estidios Medievales de Estella 19 al 23 de julio de 2010 (Pamplona, 2011), pp. 243–61.

[8] Key works on John's financial demands are J. C. Holt, *The Northerners: a Study in the Reign of King John* (Oxford, 1961), ch. 9, 'The loss of Normandy and its consequences'; N. Barratt, 'The revenue of King John', *Eng. Hist. Rev.*, cxi (1996), 835–55; and compare N. Barratt, 'The English revenue of Richard I', *Eng. Hist. Rev.*, cxvi (2001), 635–56.

of Corfe castle. As a contemporary writer put it, John was 'brimful of evil qualities'.[9]

In 1215, John was, therefore, placed beneath the law, but the Magna Carta of 1215 was very far from giving equal treatment to all the king's subjects. Socially it was a divided and divisive document, often reflecting the interests of a baronial elite a few hundred strong in a population of several million.[10] Indeed the Charter did not merely reflect social divisions: in places it was designed to reinforce them. Having asserted that taxation required the common consent of the kingdom, the assembly giving that consent was to be attended primarily by earls, barons, bishops and abbots. There was no place for London and other towns, although the Londoners thought that there should be. There was no place for knights elected by and representing the counties. In other words, there was no equivalent of the house of commons.

At least, in the chapter on taxation, the good and great of the realm could be seen as protecting the rest of the king's subjects from arbitrary exactions. But the king's subjects were far from sharing equally in the Charter's benefits. Indeed, the unfree villeins, who made up perhaps half the population, did not formally share in those benefits at all.[11] The liberties in the Charter were granted not to 'all the men' of the kingdom, but to 'all the free men'. The most famous chapter of Magna Carta, one of those still on the Statute Book, reads

> No free man is to be arrested, or imprisoned, or dispossessed, or outlawed, or exiled, or in any way destroyed, nor will we go against him, nor will we send against him, save by the lawful judgement of his peers or by the law of the land.

It is, therefore, only 'freemen' who are preserved from arbitrary arrest and dispossession. As far as Magna Carta was concerned, both king and lords remained perfectly free to dispossess their unfree tenants at will. The threat of doing so was a vital weapon for control of the peasant workforce.

The next chapter, likewise still on the Statute Book, seemed more universal.

> 'To *no one* will we deny, delay or sell right or justice'.

---

[9] Carpenter, *Magna Carta*, pp. 79–80. There are three fine biographies of King John: W.L. Warren, *King John* (new edn., New Haven and London, 1997); S. Church, *King John: England, Magna Carta and the Making of a Tyrant* (2015) and M. Morris, *King John: Treachery, Tyranny and the Road to Magna Carta* (2015).

[10] For this theme, see chapters 4 and 5 of Carpenter, *Magna Carta*.

[11] For the law relating to villeins in this period, see P. R. Hyams, *King, Lords and Peasants in Medieval England: the Common Law of Villeinage in the Twelfth and Thirteenth Centuries* (Oxford, 1980), an absolutely groundbreaking book.

But this was less helpful to the unfree than it seemed. It was the law itself which laid down that villeins had no access to the king's courts in any matter concerning their land and services. These were entirely for the lord to determine. As one law book put it, a villein when he wakes up in the morning does not know what services he must perform for his lord by night.[12] The one chapter in the Charter which specifically protected the unfree was less than it seemed. Under chapter 20 fines imposed on villeins were to match the offence and be assessed by local men. During the negotiations at Runnymede, this chapter was redrafted to make it clear that the fines in question were those imposed by the king. In other words, they did not apply to fines imposed by lords. Lords were protecting their villeins from the king so they could take all the more themselves.

Magna Carta's attitude to women was more nuanced. An important chapter protected widows from being forced into remarriage. Chapter 39 referred to the 'free man' but 'man' could be understood to mean 'human being'.[13] Indeed, the chapter probably owed something to the way John had 'destroyed' Matilda de Briouze. The Charter, however, also reflected the inequalities between men and women. It gives the names of thirty-four men, while three women are mentioned: John's queen, and the sisters of King Alexander II of Scotland. Not one was named. This was but part and parcel of the limited role women played in public life. If a free woman secured judgement of peers under the terms of chapter 39, those peers would have been entirely male, for women did not sit on juries. Chapter 39 also forgot about women altogether when it spoke of outlawry, for rather than being outlawed women were 'waived', which meant left as a 'waif'. This had the same effect. A waived woman could be killed on sight just like an outlawed man. But the distinction showed how subject women were to men. Women took no oath of allegiance to the king because in theory they were always under the protection of a man – father, husband or lord. They were, therefore, never 'in law' and so could not be 'outlawed', hence they were 'waived' instead. The only chapter (54) of the Charter where the word 'woman' ('femina') appears was designed to put women on a lower plane than men when making accusations of homicide. The implication was that women could not be trusted.

It is easy, therefore, to dismiss Magna Carta as a 'feudal' document, in which selfish baronial men looked after their own interests at the expense of the great bulk of the population. Such a view has been powerfully

[12] *Bracton on the Laws and Customs of England*, ed. G. E. Woodbine, translated with revisions and notes by S. E. Thorne (4 vols., Cambridge, Mass., 1968–77), ii. 89.

[13] See *The Treatise on the Laws and Customs of England commonly called Glanvill*, ed. G. D. G. Hall (1965), p. 106, a reference I owe to John Gillingham.

argued during the Charter's 800th anniversary commemorations, yet it is misleading. Magna Carta had a much broader appeal. Chapter 1 protected the freedom of the church. Chapters 12 and 13 protected the liberties of London and other towns. Chapters 18 and 48 gave an important role to knights, elected in the county courts, in administering justice and reforming local government. The chapters facilitating litigation under the procedures of the common law benefited all free men (around half the population). Indeed these chapters actually cut across the interests of great barons since they undermined the jurisdictions of their own courts. The numerous chapters repressing the malpractices of the king's local agents – his sheriffs, castellans and bailiffs – had considerable benefits even for the unfree. Magna Carta thus responded to the grievances of wide sections of society. Had it not done so it would never have survived.

In 1215 itself any survival appeared problematic. Within a few months of its promulgation the Charter seemed a failure without a future. John had got the pope to quash it. The barons had likewise abandoned it. They deposed John and elected another king in his place, none other than Prince Louis, the eldest son of the king of France. Louis had no brief for the Charter, and on his arrival in England in May 1216, said nothing about it. Magna Carta only survived because of John's death in October 1216. The minority government of his son, the nine-year-old Henry III, in a desperate situation with Louis controlling over half the country, decided on a complete change of course. They accepted what John had rejected and Louis was ignoring. In November 1216, they issued, in the young king's name, a new version of Magna Carta.[14] Having won the war, in part because of this concession, they issued a second version of the Charter in November 1217 as part of the peace settlement. Then, in 1225, in order to secure a great tax, Henry III issued what became the final and definitive Magna Carta. It is chapters of Henry III's Charter of 1225, not John's of 1215, which remain on the Statute Book today. Indeed in the thirteenth century it was Henry's Charter of 1225 which was called 'Magna Carta'. John's Charter of 1215 was more often called just 'the Charter of Runnymede'. The name 'Magna Carta' itself had only appeared in 1218 to distinguish the 'Great Charter' from the physically smaller Charter dealing with the royal forest which Henry III issued alongside it. It was not until the seventeenth century that John's Charter recovered its place centre stage and became called Magna Carta.

It is sometimes said that in its first century Magna Carta was little more than 'guff'. It asserted high principles but had little practical effect. Recent

---

[14] For a catalogue of the new versions of the Charter with illustrations of the surviving originals, see Vincent, *Magna Carta: Origins and Legacy*, pp. 204–71.

research shows this view to be wrong. In the first place the Charter was far more than just a vague symbol of good government. Its detail was immensely well known. This had started in 1215 itself. It used to be thought that in 1215 originals of Magna Carta were sent to the sheriffs in charge of the counties, so there was one for every county. In fact, evidence is building up to show that the Charters were sent not to the sheriffs but to the bishops and their cathedrals. Two of the four surviving originals have been at cathedrals – Lincoln and Salisbury – throughout their life. An exciting discovery has shown that another of the originals (one of the two now in the British Library) was once at Canterbury Cathedral where it almost certainly went in 1215.[15] In the great British Library Magna Carta exhibition it was described as the 'Canterbury Magna Carta'. For John's opponents the bishops and their cathedrals were far safer depositories of the Charter than the sheriffs and their castles; after all the sheriffs were the very people under attack in the Charter. Had Magna Carta been sent to them it would soon have disappeared into their castle furnaces. The bishops, on the other hand, with the first chapter of the Charter protecting the liberties of the church, had every reason to preserve and proclaim it.

The originals at the cathedrals were not the only source of knowledge of the 1215 Charter. New research has also shown that numerous unofficial copies were circulated round the country.[16] Many of these were not of the final authorized text and derived instead from drafts produced during the negotiations at Runnymede. This spreading knowledge on the Charter helps explain its survival. From the start it was digging deep roots into the hearts and minds of the political community. That was why the minority government of Henry III took the crucial decision to revive it. Copies of the 1215 Charter continued to be made throughout the thirteenth century. Equally copied were the Charters of 1217 and 1225. Such copies are found in chronicles, cartularies and legal collections made by lawyers. The chapters were often numbered, described and analysed, with the differences between the different versions being pointed out.

By the end of the century, Magna Carta in its various forms was known in all strata of society. In 1300 it was proclaimed in English, the language of the general run of the population. Around the same time it was appealed to by

---

[15] Carpenter, *Magna Carta*, pp. 477–80. The hypothesis that the originals of the 1215 Charter were sent to cathedrals was first developed by I. W. Rowlands, 'The text and distribution of the writ for the publication of Magna Carta, 1215', *Eng. Hist. Rev.*, cxxiv (2009), 1422–31.

[16] See the section 'Copies of Magna Carta' on the website of the Magna Carta project <http://www.magnacartaresearch.org> [accessed 22 March 2018].

the peasants of Bocking in Essex, later a centre of the peasants' revolt.[17] The Charter had also effected a profound change in the workings of monarchy. Stopping up many arbitrary sources of revenue, and insisting that general taxation required common consent, it had helped create the tax-based parliamentary state. It was a real watershed between lawless and lawful rule. It had established the base from which it would later go round the world.

[17] Carpenter, *Magna Carta*, pp. 435, 457–8.

3. Magna Carta: from King John to western liberty*

Nicholas Vincent

On 15 June 2015, the 800th anniversary of the sealing of Magna Carta, leaders of the British establishment gathered in the field of Runnymede, on the banks of the river Thames, twenty or so miles west of London. The queen and the duke of Edinburgh were there. So was the duke of Cambridge (future heir to the British throne), the archbishop of Canterbury (Justin Welby), the prime minister (David Cameron) and a large number of government, military and civic dignitaries. The attorney general of the United States of America (Loretta Lynch) attended as a representative of President Obama. Together she and the Princess Royal, Princess Anne, re-inaugurated the American Bar Association memorial on the field of Runnymede: a classical rotunda, built in 1957, decorated with American stars and housing a pedestal that declares its dedication to 'Magna Carta, symbol of freedom under law'.

A neutral observer might be forgiven for considering this a most peculiar occasion. Why, for example, were so many members of the British royal family involved in the commemoration of a document that so severely limited the exercise of royal power? Why were there as many American as there were British spectators? What did it say about the conservatism of the British 'establishment' that the archbishop of Canterbury travelled to Runnymede from his London residence at Lambeth, just as his predecessor, Stephen Langton, had done in June 1215, and that the queen arrived from her castle at Windsor, just as King John had done in 1215, albeit transported by helicopter rather than on horseback? As for the celebrations themselves, they were described to me as 'a magnificent blend of fascist flag rally and boy scout jamboree'. Certainly, they seemed to have little to do with the real history of the document, King John's Magna Carta, whose anniversary was celebrated.

Magna Carta has passed through many centennials. Yet it is surely significant for our understanding of British history that the anniversary of

---

* One version of this paper has been published in Chinese. Others were published in Armenian, by the University of Yerevan, and in French under the auspices of the Université de Paris and the Université de Lille.

N. Vincent, 'Magna Carta: from King John to western liberty', in *Magna Carta: history, context and influence*, ed. L. Goldman (2018), pp. 25–40.

2015 should have been the first to have been so elaborately stage-managed. On the 500th anniversary, in 1715, the British paid little attention to Magna Carta, being too involved in Jacobite Rebellion. In 1815, Napoleon stole the show, obliging the British army to return to Flanders, on the eve of its great test at Waterloo (18 June). In 1915, the British army was once again in Flanders and celebrations of Magna Carta, in preparation since 1913, were cancelled in the face of German aerial bombardment of London, the second battle of Ypres, the sinking of the Lusitania and the Allied landings at Gallipoli. As this should demonstrate, and for all its 800-year history, whatever else it may have done, Magna Carta has brought the British no relief from foreign wars, nor from political turmoil that as recently as 1715, and again after 1815 and 1915 (not least in Ireland), threatened to develop into revolutionary chaos.

Referring to Magna Carta on 4 July 1918, with the end of the First World War in sight, Winston Churchill declared that the American Declaration of Independence 'follows on the Magna Charta and the Bill of Rights (1689) as the third great title-deed on which the liberties of the English-speaking people are founded'.[1] His words were intended to celebrate the wartime alliance between Britain and America, cemented by a new 'English-Speaking Union'. Yet were they anything more than empty rhetoric? Certainly, they have since been repeated by countless politicians around the world. Why such praise for a document that even today, in its 800th anniversary year, very few people have read and even fewer can claim properly to understand?

Magna Carta is celebrated today as one of the foundation stones of constitutionalism throughout the English-speaking world: an 800-year-old guarantee of the rule of law. In origin, however, it had no such universal meaning. At is most basic, it is an 800-year-old peace treaty made between the king and his leading subjects, the 'barons' of England. Four copies issued officially from the chancery of King John still survive. Two of these 'originals' of the 1215 Magna Carta are preserved in the British Library in London, the two others in the cathedral archives of Salisbury and Lincoln.[2] The treaty records an attempt by barons and king, in the summer of 1215, to put an end to a civil war itself the product of the king's incompetence and tyranny. King John (1199–1215) came to the throne as the youngest son of the great Henry II (1154–89). Founder of the Angevin 'empire' in

---

[1] P. Clark, *Mr Churchill's Profession: Statesman, Orator, Writer* (2012), p. xv and cf. pp. 81, 106, 110–11.

[2] Studies here include J. C. Holt, *Magna Carta* (Cambridge, 1st edn. 1965; 2nd edn. 1992; 3rd edn. 2015); D. Carpenter, *Magna Carta* (2015); N. Vincent, *Magna Carta: a Very Short Introduction* (Oxford, 2012), and (with illustrations of each one of the surviving 24 original Magna Cartas) N. Vincent, *Magna Carta: Origins and Legacy* (Oxford, 2016).

France, Henry II had been a ruler on a truly imperial scale. Ruling more French territory than any king since the collapse of the Carolingian dynasty, 300 years before, he had not only extended his dominion by conquests in Ireland and Brittany, but ensured its commemoration in literary and architectural memorials worthy to stand alongside those of the court of Charlemagne as a self-consciously magnificent celebration of the rise of empire. John's greatest failing was his inability to live up to the reputation either of his empire-building father, Henry II, or of his heroic elder brother, the crusader king, Richard 'Lionheart' (1189–99).[3]

Kings in the middle ages were expected to discharge two chief functions: they were to maintain and if possible extend the frontiers of their dominion, and guard their subjects against foreign attack. In the process, they were also to ensure that justice was done and that the rights and property of their inferiors were protected. It is precisely these functions that were proclaimed on the great seals of King John and his ancestors: the means by which the king himself authenticated his own letters and laws. On one side, the great seal showed the king on horseback riding into battle. On the other, it portrayed him enthroned in majesty, with the orb of dominion and the sword of justice, ruling his people as God's chosen instrument on earth.[4] In both of these functions, military and judicial, John proved a miserable failure. In 1202, he faced rebellion from his young nephew, the fifteen-year-old Arthur of Brittany. Such rebellion was nothing new. Indeed it had become a more or less regular feature of the family politics of John and his ancestors, the Plantagenet kings. Through a lightning raid and with considerable aplomb, John took Arthur prisoner. So far so good. This was the fate of many previous royal rebels, locked away, blinded or castrated as a means of invalidating their claims to power. But in Arthur's case, things went seriously wrong.

In circumstances that still remain mysterious, Arthur simply disappeared. He was last heard of at Falaise, or possibly Rouen, within a few days of his capture. Some alleged that he thereafter died attempting escape. Others that he was murdered by the king in a fit of drunken rage. Most likely, he was killed or starved to death at the king's command. To imprison a kinsman was one thing; to kill him quite another. The act branded King John for ever afterwards as a tyrant, slayer of his own flesh and blood, the killer moreover of a boy barely out of puberty, fit candidate to be celebrated as an innocent martyr. The barons of northern France, tired of endless

[3] For John, there are good biographies by S. Painter, *The Reign of King John* (Baltimore, Md., 1949); W. L. Warren, *King John* (New Haven, Conn., 1961), and S. Church, *King John: England, Magna Carta and the Making of a Tyrant* (2015).

[4] Image in Vincent, *Magna Carta: Origins and Legacy*, p. 200.

wars between the kings of England and their rivals in Paris, threw in their lot with King Philip of France. Philip invaded Normandy. John fled to England. Within the space of only two years, the entire Plantagenet empire north of the river Loire was lost to Philip and the French.[5]

John was determined to reconquer these lost lands. To that end, he raised a vast war chest through taxation and the exploitation of his feudal rights. Previously to a large extent an absentee from England, he now resided for the most part in London and the southern counties, a constant threat to his English barons, eyeing up not only their financial resources but their wives and daughters. The king was a notorious lecher. He was also notoriously cruel. After 1210, he is said to have starved to death the wife and eldest son of one of his leading barons, William de Briouze: a man who had previously stood among John's closest friends, but whom he abandoned, disgraced and hounded into exile. As with Arthur, the persecution of the Briouzes supplied the king's enemies with what must have seemed a God-given opportunity to blacken John's name.[6] Nor was it only the barons from whom a backlash came.

The king sprang from a family whose relations with the Church had never been smooth. In 1170, John's father, Henry II, had notoriously spoken out against the then archbishop of Canterbury, Thomas Becket, provoking Becket's murder in Canterbury Cathedral. Ever afterwards, however blameless they might claim to be for the martyrdom of 'St. Thomas', the Plantagenet dynasty was branded in the eyes of the pope and the Church as a dynasty of murderers, the sons of Belial, the Devil's Brood (from the verdict upon Henry II pronounced by St. Bernard, c.1152, 'From the Devil he came, and to the Devil he will surely return').[7] As a result, after 1205, when King John attempted to have one of his henchmen promoted as archbishop of Canterbury, the pope refused. Instead, John was commanded to accept as archbishop a man, Stephen Langton, who although born in England had spent the past thirty years in Paris. There Langton had lectured on the Bible, drawing comparisons between the good and bad kings of the present day, the Plantagenets included, and

---

[5] For the 'empire', building upon the work of J. C. Holt, 'The end of the Anglo-Norman realm', *Proc. Brit. Acad.*, lxi (1975), 223–65, see J. Gillingham, *The Angevin Empire* (2nd edn., 2001); D. Power, *The Norman Frontier in the Twelfth and Early Thirteenth Centuries* (Cambridge, 2004).

[6] D. Crouch, 'Baronial paranoia in King John's reign', and 'The complaint of King John against William de Briouze', in *Magna Carta and the England of King John*, ed. J.S. Loengard (Woodbridge, 2010), pp. 45–62, 168–79.

[7] References in N. Vincent, 'The seals of King Henry II and his court', in *Seals and their Context in the Middle Ages*, ed. P. R. Schofield (Oxford, 2015), pp. 15, 28 fn.78.

the tyrants and heroes whose exploits were described in the Christian Old Testament.[8]

John refused to accept Langton. The pope refused to abandon him. The outcome, from 1208 to 1213, was a stand-off between Church and state. Throughout this period of 'Interdict', the mass and other sacraments were not publicly celebrated; the dead were not buried in consecrated ground; the king's court was excommunicated, and the king himself was threatened not just with excommunication but the possibility that the pope might now back an invasion of England by the French king Philip Augustus, deposing John and placing his greatest rival upon the English throne. To avoid such an eventuality, in 1213, John backed down. The pope was promised titular lordship over both England and Ireland together with an annual 'census' or rent (a token sum of £666, 1,000 'marks'). In return, the pope now treated John as a favoured son.[9]

Using the vast treasure that he had by now extracted, both from his barons and from the confiscated property of the Church, John embarked on a campaign of reconquest in France. This ended in catastrophe at the battle of Bouvines, fought outside Lille, on 27 July 1214. Here John's northern allies, including the Holy Roman Emperor, Otto IV, were decisively defeated by Philip of France. John himself, who was south of the Loire at the time, was obliged to slink back to England for the second time in his reign, defeated in war and with his treasury exhausted.

The outcome was rebellion and civil war. In the hope of cementing the friendship of the pope, John himself took vows as a crusader. This in theory placed him under the direct protection of the Church. In the meantime, a large number of English barons, particularly those of East Anglia and the North, rose up against the king.[10] They enjoyed the tacit support of Langton and other English bishops, many of whom had financial or personal grievances of their own against John, arising from the problems of the Interdict since 1208. From among this opposition party – a truly political coalition between barons and clerics, one of the first such in English history – voices began to be raised demanding that John reissue the promises made by earlier kings to rule well and in accordance with custom and law. In

---

[8] The classic biography of Langton remains that by F. M. Powicke, *Stephen Langton* (Oxford, 1928), although see more recently P. Buc, *L'Ambiguité du livre: prince, pouvoir, et peuple dans les commentaires de la Bible au Moyen Age* (Paris, 1994), and various of the essays, especially those by Baldwin and Vincent, collected in *Etienne Langton: prédicateur, bibliste, théologien*, ed. L.-J. Bataillon, N. Beriou, G. Dahan and R. Quinto (Turnhout, 2010).

[9] C. R. Cheney, *Pope Innocent III and England* (Stuttgart, 1976), pp. 303–56.

[10] For the roots of the rebellion, the classic study remains J. C. Holt, *The Northerners: a Study in the Reign of King John* (Oxford, 1961; 2nd edn. 1992).

particular, attention was drawn, perhaps by Langton, perhaps by others, to the so-called 'Coronation Charter' that John's great-grandfather, King Henry I, had issued in 1100. Here, at a desperate moment in his own career, Henry I had been persuaded to limit the extent of royal exploitation of feudal rights over widows, orphans and the Church.[11] Let King John, the barons now demanded, reissue this charter, suitably updated so as to answer the circumstances of 1215.

In May 1215, the city of London, itself tired of the king's financial exploitation and disgruntled with French wars that placed an embargo on foreign trade, threw in its lot with the rebels. The king was now forced to negotiate. At Runnymede, on and around 15 June 1215, at a location halfway between the royal castle at Windsor and the rebel stronghold in London, John met with the rebel barons and agreed a settlement, based in part upon Henry I's coronation charter, in part upon more recent developments. Runnymede was chosen as a liminal spot, on the banks of the Thames, neither entirely land nor water, at a place where the boundaries of four English counties met, and perhaps more significantly the boundaries of four English dioceses (the bishoprics of Lincoln, London, Winchester and Salisbury).[12]

The document thrashed out at Runnymede, known to us as Magna Carta, was first and foremost a peace treaty. Its intention was to place limitations upon the king's power both to tax and to trouble his subjects, in order that peace might be re-established between king and realm. Thus, among its sixty or more provisions, it included clauses on the liberties of the Church, of the city of London, and above all protecting the customary rights of the barons, their heirs and dependents. It included much else besides.[13] For example, it sought to promote peace between England, Scotland and Wales (clauses 56–9). It decreed standard measures for wine, corn and cloth (clause 35, significantly calculated according to the measures already adopted by the city of London). It sought to prevent any resurgence in royal authority, first by calling for the expulsion of a list of the king's named foreign constables (clauses 50–1), and thereafter by imposing a supervisory

[11] For the text of Henry I's coronation charter as received by barons and king in 1215, see Holt, *Magna Carta* (1965), pp. 296–303; Carpenter, *Magna Carta*, pp. 310–15.

[12] For the site, see T. Tatton-Brown, 'Magna Carta at 800: uncovering its landscape archaeology', *Current Archaeology*, cciv (July 2015), 34–7, also of importance for demonstrating that the medieval 'Runnymede' is almost certainly not included within the land currently managed by the National Trust, representing what in the middle ages was known as 'Long Meadow'.

[13] For the text, see Holt, *Magna Carta* (1965), pp. 316–37; Vincent, *Magna Carta: a Very Short Introduction*, pp. 111–24; Carpenter, *Magna Carta*, pp. 36–69.

committee of twenty-five barons above and over the king (clause 61, the so-called 'security clause'). These men were in effect empowered to make war against John should the king in any way infringe the terms of the Charter.

The choice of the number twenty-five here suggests the influence of the archbishop of Canterbury, Stephen Langton, since it was in theology and biblical exegesis that the number twenty-five was widely advertized as a number appropriate to the law (being five times five, or the square of the number of books of law in the Old Testament, the so-called Pentateuch).[14] Other clauses of the Charter, far from being pure 'English' law, were so close to expedients attempted elsewhere in France or northern Spain as to suggest a degree of conscious imitation of continental precedents. In particular, several clauses of Magna Carta, on the liberties of the Church, on free access to justice, on inheritance, the rights of widows and orphans and so forth, were anticipated in the so-called 'Statute of Pamiers' issued in 1212 by the French baron, Simon de Montfort, for his subjects in those parts of Toulouse and southern France recently conquered in the Albigensian Crusade. Magna Carta did not simply copy Pamiers. Both settlements nonetheless reflected tensions between rulers and the ruled, shared across wide areas of Europe in the decades either side of 1215.[15]

Rather surprisingly for a settlement that is supposed to have been 'radical' and to have introduced nothing but good, the 1215 Magna Carta also contains clauses that today seem deeply reactionary or contrary to modern ideas of justice and right. Thus it is firm in its condemnation of the usury charged by Jews against the debts of underage heirs (clauses 10–11); in its limitation of the access to justice allowed to women (clause 54); and in its demand for the expulsion of foreigners (clauses 50–1, here described as 'aliens', borrowing a word used in the Old Testament book of Maccabees to describe outsiders in occupation of the Holy Land). In only a few places does the Charter enunciate what might be described as general or legal principles. In clause 60, for instance, it demands that the customs and liberties hereby guaranteed by the king to his barons be extended by the barons to all lesser men: an essential widening of the settlement, that transformed it from being a narrowly 'feudal' document, of benefit to the few, into a much more generous concession, available to the many.

---

[14] N. Vincent, 'The twenty-five barons of Magna Carta: an Augustinian echo?', in *Rulership and Rebellion in the Anglo-Norman World, c.1066–c.1216: Essays in Honour of Professor Edmund King*, ed. P. Dalton and D. Luscombe (Farnham, 2015), pp. 231–51.

[15] N. Vincent, 'English liberties, Magna Carta (1215) and the Spanish connection', in *1212–1214: El trienio que hizo a Europa*, Acta de la XXXVII Semana de Estidios Medievales de Estella 19 al 23 de julio de 2010 (Pamplona, 2011), pp. 243–61.

Most famously, clauses 39 and 40 of the Charter enunciate a general principle that in England we would describe as the rule of law, or in America as the right to 'due process':

> No free man is to be arrested, or imprisoned, or disseised, or outlawed, or exiled, or in any other way ruined, nor will we go against him or send against him, except by the lawful judgment of his peers or by the law of the land.

> We will not sell, or deny, or delay right or justice to anyone

Together with clauses 1 and 13 on the freedom of the Church and the liberties of the city of London, these two clauses are the only fragments of Magna Carta that still remain law in England today. They have been widely imitated, so that echoes of them are to be found in the American Bill of Rights, in the French Declaration of the Rights of Man (1789) and in the 1948 United Nations Universal Declaration of Human Rights. Yet we should notice, from the start, how vague they become whenever we attempt to pin them down to specific points of law. Who, for example, is a free man? Did this category include both women and men (answer: for the most part yes), and did it exclude the vast majority of the population who, in 1215, would have been considered servile peasants living without the right of appeal to the king's courts (answer: probably no)? We are to be judged by our 'peers', that is to say by our equals (the term *pares* in Latin here being borrowed from the French word *pair*, as in the modern 'pair of aces' in a game of cards). But who are our equals? Are the rich to be judged by the poor, or those of aristocratic birth by mere commoners? Moreover, what is the 'law of the land' by which 'lawful judgement' is to be obtained? In 1215, indeed until as late as the 19th century, there was no single book to which one could refer in England in which the 'law of the land' was clearly and concisely set out. Rather, law was a matter not just of statute but of custom, process and to some extent of expediency. Moreover, who was to determine whether any particular judgement was or was not 'lawful'?

Here, bizarrely, we return to the sovereign power of the king as the only authority capable of determining what was or was not to be considered 'lawful judgement'. Magna Carta as a whole, framed as an act of grace, granted by the king to his barons, bishops and other subjects, enshrines the principle that it is the king who delivers justice, grants privileges, and ultimately has the power both to extend and to limit the authority of the law. Far from placing the king under the law, Magna Carta can in this reading appear a document that promotes the king as lawgiver. No wonder, perhaps, that so many members of the British royal family queued up in 2015 to celebrate the Charter's anniversary.

Furthermore, as granted in 1215, it was clear from the very start that the charter agreed at Runnymede would provoke outrage and repudiation. The king was a feudal subject of the pope. Yet the Charter deliberately ignored the pope's rights as overlord, specifically forbidding the king from seeking adjudication from any higher authority. The king in theory derived his powers from God, yet the Charter attempted to insert a committee of twenty-five barons as judges over the king. No such settlement could be accepted either by pope or by king. In medieval conceptualization, the king was head of the body politic. How could any authority, papal or royal, permit the head to be ruled by the body's inferior members? It is worth noticing that, even when they invited the king of France to invade England and support them against King John, the barons made no attempt to persuade King Philip, or Louis, his son, that Magna Carta was something worth reissuing or defending. This was a document as repugnant to the kings of France as it was to the pope or King John. Within twelve weeks of its issue, the peace that it sought to establish had irrevocably collapsed. The barons refused to surrender the city of London. The king refused to expel his alien sheriffs and constables. In August, the pope declared the Charter annulled.[16] In September, king and barons once again went to war against each other. After barely twelve weeks, Magna Carta expired: a failed treaty that brought war rather than peace.

For the next year, the king made war on his barons with barely a thought for what had been negotiated at Runnymede. To lead their cause, the barons encouraged Louis, eldest son of King Philip of France, to lead a French invasion of England. But in October 1216, King John died, struck down, we are told, by an attack of dysentery contracted from eating peaches and new cider. The throne now passed to his son, a nine-year-old boy, the future King Henry III. With Louis ruling in London, and threatening now to seek coronation in Westminster Abbey, the traditional site of such ceremonies, Henry III's ministers not only had their boy king crowned at Gloucester, far away in the west, but a few days later, at Bristol, reissued Magna Carta. The charter was now offered as a manifesto of future good government, to persuade the realm that Henry would in future rule better than his father had done. In the process, about a third of its length and many of its more radical clauses were pruned away. Out went the clauses on consent for taxation. Out went those on aliens or the Jews. Above all, out went the so-called 'security clause' by which the king at Runnymede had bound himself to observe the advice and authority of a committee of twenty-five barons.

---

[16] Cheney, *Pope Innocent III and England*, pp. 382–6.

What remained, including the guarantees of due process and of the liberties of the Church, of London, of the barons and the freemen of England, was first reissued by Henry III in November 1216, sealed not only by the king's chief guardian, William Marshal earl of Pembroke, but by the pope's local representative, the legate Guala Bicchieri, a native of Vercelli in northern Italy. By this means, the Charter was henceforth endorsed not just by the king's ministers but, in effect, by the papacy, God's highest representative on earth. Again sealed by the legate, the Charter was reissued once the civil war had been won by the king's party in November 1217. It was issued again in 1225, when Henry III came of age, now in a definitive form whose text was to change only in minor details thereafter. It was the 1225 version of the Charter that henceforth was treated as law. The peace treaty of 1215 was thus transformed into a statute. Reissued again in 1234, in 1253, in 1265, after 1272, in 1297 and for a last time in 1300, the Charter of 1225 achieved totemic status.[17] By 1300, indeed as early as the 1250s, many of the terms of the Charter were anachronistic, divorced from the day-to-day concerns of political society. What mattered were not the individual clauses on inheritance, widows, wards or financial obligations, but the fact that the charter had come to be regarded as something approaching holy writ, widely believed to protect the king's subjects, their liberties and their sense of communal right against the threat of royal tyranny.[18] Although grounded in the absolute sovereignty of the crown, the Charter was perceived as in some senses a concession to popular right. Granted by 'We the king', rather than 'We the people', it nonetheless recognized a degree of mutual dependence in dealings between ruler and ruled.

It had also increasingly come to be associated with an institution that had emerged since the 1230s from a more ancient tradition of councils and representative assemblies summoned by English kings. Now described as 'parliaments' ('speaking togethers'), the more solemn meetings of the king's councillors were by the 1250s capable not only of convening in the king's absence but of incorporating representatives of the localities, sent to such 'parliaments' both to air local grievances and to discuss the granting of tax. Following a renewal of hostilities between king and barons between 1258 and 1265, parliament was both institutionalized and transformed into a theatre of kingship. In the hands of Henry III's son, Edward I, king of England from

[17] For the various reissues, see F. Thompson, *The First Century of Magna Carta: Why it Persisted as a Document* (Minneapolis, Minn., 1925); Vincent, *Magna Carta: Origins and Legacy*, pp. 206–56.

[18] J. R. Maddicott, 'Magna Carta and the local community, 1215–1259', *Past & Present*, cii (1984), 25–65.

1272–1307, it was summoned to display royal magnanimity and justice.[19] Nonetheless, by this time the idea had been firmly planted that kingship was itself conditional upon royal respect and service to the community of the realm. In particular, the financial problems of the English crown, and the inability of kings to finance their own wars in France without taxation from their people, guaranteed parliament, at times of crisis, a political role quite unlike that enjoyed by the more supine representative assemblies of kingdoms such as France or the Holy Roman Empire.[20] Elsewhere in Europe, kings never fully acknowledged the right of such assemblies to veto taxation or supply. In England, they had little choice but to accept such limits.[21] This too might be seen as a consequence of Magna Carta which, by limiting the traditional extortions of royal government, rendered future reliance on parliamentary taxation more or less inevitable.

Once again, it is important to remember that England in the later middle ages was not in any material sense better ruled than other nations. Good and bad kings came and went. In contrast to other nations, the English gained notoriety for their willingness to depose and ultimately to kill their kings: Edward II in 1327, Richard II in 1399, Henry VI deposed from 1461 to 1470, killed in 1471, Richard III, killed in battle in 1485. There is little to suggest that the warlords and churchmen who presided over such killings had any more fundamental belief in popular sovereignty or the rights of the people than the warlords and bishops of France or Germany. Much of the turmoil of late medieval English politics was circumstantial and emerged from a combination of the personal incompetence of royalty, the pressures of war and finance, and the structural weaknesses both of central and local government. There is nothing in this to suggest that Magna Carta, although continually reconfirmed in parliament and used for the training of lawyers, placed at the head of many thousands of laboriously copied books of statutes, was in any sense responsible for English exceptionalism. It did nonetheless enshrine the principal that limitations upon monarchy lay at the root of English law, embedding such concepts as 'liberty', 'custom' and 'right' deep within the English political consciousness.[22]

[19] J. R. Maddicott, 'Edward I and the lessons of baronial reform: local government, 1258–80', in *Thirteenth Century England I*, ed. P. R. Coss and S. D. Lloyd (Woodbridge, 1986), pp. 1–30.

[20] J. C. Holt, 'The prehistory of parliament', in *The English Parliament in the Middle Ages*, ed R. G. Davies and J. H. Denton (Manchester, 1981), pp. 1–28; J. R. Maddicott, *The Origins of the English Parliament 924–1327* (Oxford, 2010).

[21] G. L. Harriss, *King, Parliament and Public Finance in Medieval England to 1369* (Oxford, 1975).

[22] F. Thompson, *Magna Carta: its Role in the Making of the English Constitution 1300–1629* (Minneapolis, Minn., 1948), pp. 9–136; J. H. Baker, *The Reinvention of Magna Carta 1216–*

The subsequent reinventions of Magna Carta can be only briefly touched on here. With the fading away of serfdom, the idea of the 'free man' came to define not just the rich but the majority of England's population, rich and poor, male and female. The rights guaranteed under Magna Carta clauses 39 and 40 thus became available to all. As such, they were loudly trumpeted throughout the period of political crisis between king and nation in the seventeenth century, culminating in the execution of Charles I in 1649, and the expulsion of his son, James II, in 1688.[23] By this time, Magna Carta was not so much read as mythologized. It had become a liberty document, believed in some vague way to uphold an age-old tradition of protection under the law for those opposing the arbitrary powers of the king.[24] It was as such that it crossed the Atlantic in the seventeenth century, carried to America almost as a genetic birthright of the settlers established in the new colonies of Virginia, Maryland, Jamaica and elsewhere. Hence, from the 1760s onwards, the way in which Magna Carta was employed by the colonists to argue their right to representation, to freedom from arbitrary burdens or arrest, and to possession of those liberties claimed for all freeborn subjects of the British crown, in this instance no longer as an anti-royal instrument so much as a check upon the powers of an over-mighty parliament.[25] To this phase of Magna Carta's history there was as much make-believe and misunderstanding as there was sound history. A true understanding of the Charter's purpose became overlaid by a desire to view it as a universal panacea.[26]

It is from such readings that many of the present misconceptions of the document emerge. It is today widely supposed that Magna Carta underpins a whole series of liberties peculiarly associated with English law. Democracy, parliament, 'habeas corpus', presumption of innocence in criminal trials,

---

1616 (Cambridge, 2017), and for European comparisons, J. Watts, *The Making of Polities: Europe, 1300–1500* (Cambridge, 2009).

[23] In general, for English exceptionalism, see A. Macfarlane, *The Origins of English Individualism* (Oxford, 1978). For Magna Carta after 1500, see Thompson, *Magna Carta: its Role*, pp. 139–374.

[24] J. Champion, 'From *Liber Homo* to "free-born Englishman": how Magna Carta became a "liberty document", 1508–1760s', in *Magna Carta: the Foundation of Freedom, 1215–2015*, ed. N. Vincent (2014), pp. 103–18.

[25] A. E. Dick Howard, *The Road from Runnymede: Magna Carta and Constitutionalism in America* (Charlottesville, Va., 1968); J. L. Malcolm, 'Magna Carta in America: entrenched', in Vincent, *Magna Carta: the Foundation of Freedom*, pp. 121–35.

[26] For the later history, see A. Pallister, *Magna Carta: the Heritage of Liberty* (Oxford, 1971); P. Linebaugh, *The Magna Carta Manifesto: Liberties and Commons for All* (Berkeley, Calif., 2008); M. Taylor and N. Vincent, in Vincent, *Magna Carta: the Foundations of Freedom*, pp. 137–69; Vincent, *Magna Carta: Origins and Legacy*, pp. 85–150.

all of these things and more have in some way come to be attributed to a document that, in reality, deals with none of them. Even so, Magna Carta retains a surprise or two.

Take, for example, clause 33 of the 1215 charter, forbidding the construction of fish weirs on the rivers Thames and Medway. Originally included as a sop to the men of London, this clause was not in fact removed from the English statute book until 1970. Even now it continues to surface in English and Irish courts as perhaps the most frequently litigated clause in the entire document. The reason here is that clause 33 enunciates not just an archaic prejudice against fish weirs (a sort of trap made by driving wooden stakes into the bed of a river) but a principle, that navigation should be free and that certain types of property, in this case the navigable part of a river, should be considered public rather than private, as 'res publica' or, in terms that modern lawyers would understand, as rights according to 'natural law'.[27] Clauses 41 and 42 of the 1215 charter (in the case of clause 41 retained in the 1225 charter as clause 30) guaranteeing freedom of movement to foreign merchants, and freedom to the king's subjects to enter and leave the realm, might likewise seem merely banal. However, in countries around the world today, where such rights are by no means guaranteed, and where passports can be obtained only by those in political favour, these are clauses that have a very real and contemporary resonance.

Above all, in a contemporary context, Magna Carta should remind us both of the element of compromise involved in negotiations between the sovereign and the political community, and of the distinction to be drawn between autocracy and a society such as that of England, even as early as 1215, boasting a relatively mature plurality of powers. In various parts of the world, even today, to establish a stamp club or a village choir, let alone any more controversial organization, can itself be regarded as a political act subject to control and disapproval by the ruling authorities. Magna Carta, by contrast, emerges from a society in which special interests were already recognized to possess their own liberties, rights and customs. Many of these special interests were, even by 1215, specifically commercial rather than feudal, associated with the international trade of the city of London. Clauses 13 and 35 of the 1215 Magna Carta, for example, not only guarantee the liberties of London and all other cities and ports, but define London weights and measures as the standard to be adopted universally throughout the realm. Clauses 41–2 guarantee the freedom of movement of both native

[27] R. H. Helmholz, 'Magna Carta and the law of nations', in *Magna Carta, Religion and the Rule of Law*, ed. R. Griffith-Jones and M. Hill (Cambridge, 2015), pp. 76–7, and for the repeal of clause 33 (clause 23 of the 1225 charter), see Pallister, *Magna Carta: the Heritage of Liberty*, pp. 100–1.

and foreign merchants, save in time of open warfare. Even clause 33, on fish weirs, has a commercial aspect, given its intention to protect the navigation of the river Thames, and hence the river-born trade of London and much of southern England.

Those of us who consider ourselves fortunate to inhabit countries governed by the Anglophone tradition of law should avoid any temptation to complacency or self-congratulation. In 2015, it was all very well for English and American politicians to hold up their 800-year-old system of law for admiration in other parts of the world where due process is promised but seldom delivered, and where liberty and the rule of law are concepts manipulated more for the glorification of the powerful than for the benefit of the people at large. It should not be forgotten, even so, that for all its championing of liberty, Magna Carta did not oblige the English to rule well in Ireland or India or large parts of Africa. In Jamaica, it helped persuade British settlers that they enjoyed an equality more equal than that of others, with Magna Carta itself employed as a justification for dividing free from un-free, colonist from slave.[28] In modern America, it is not at all clear that the impulse to export democratic values has entirely been divorced from the imposition of American values, by force where necessary.[29]

Nonetheless, even the myth-making that surrounds Magna Carta has its own significance. The myths that people tell about themselves help to determine their future behaviour in the world. Nations founded upon a concept of God-given right, manifest destiny or a sacred mission to subdue and suppress all other nations through might and triumphant will tend to behave in ways different, both militarily and commercially, from nations founded upon a sense of age-old liberty triumphing over tyranny, right over might. Nations that believe themselves to possess an 800-year-old tradition of the rule of law, a sovereign authority or monarchy placed under restraint, and a dispersed plurality of powers, will behave rather differently from those where such concepts are either unknown or despised. To that extent, the celebrations of 2015, however bizarre, did indeed serve a more general purpose. A mature democracy requires compromise between ruler and ruled. It also implies respect for laws that both ruler and ruled obey. Tradition here, and an appeal to the past, can prove powerful incentives to good government past, present and future.

[28] Vincent, *Magna Carta: Origins and Legacy*, pp. 109–10, citing J. P. Greene, 'Liberty and slavery: the transfer of British liberty to the West Indies, 1627–1865', in *Exclusionary Empire: English Liberty Overseas, 1600–1900*, ed. J. P. Greene (Cambridge, 2009), pp. 56–7, 65–6.

[29] For freedom as something potentially enforced upon others, see P. Buc, *Holy War, Martyrdom, and Terror: Christianity, Violence, and the West, ca.70 C.E. to the Iraq War* (Philadelphia, Pa., 2015), esp. ch. 6, pp. 213–41.

I wrote various of the preceding remarks in January 2016, six months after the anniversary at Runnymede, and at a time when it was widely supposed that the referendum then pending on British membership of the European Union would be decided in defiance of calls for a retreat into past bigotry and isolationism. I write now, two years after Runnymede, at the end of 2017, with the referendum result declared, and with the very real prospect not just of a divorce between Britain and Europe but within the United Kingdom, between England and Scotland, and the majority of the population of Northern Ireland. As I hope to have shown here, the precedents for English withdrawal from Europe are not encouraging. The debacle of 1204, as a result of which King John was expelled from most of his French 'empire', led directly to 250 years of Anglo-French warfare, as kings of England struggled to recover their lost continental domain. It also provoked a crisis in public finances, both in England and, less well known, in Normandy whose barons and churches had previously depended heavily upon English revenues.[30] More dangerously still, the events of 1204 drove a wedge between, on the one hand, a small part of the elite determined to recover their lost lands and glory in France, and an increasingly xenophobic English nation that had never cared for the French and that possessed no French interests to recover. From this fundamental disparity sprang many of the tensions between king and realm in the two centuries after 1204. The Hundred Years War, from the 1340s onwards, was not so much a campaign for 'recovery' as for conquest, as Englishmen of all sorts combined under the crown in the congenial business of slaughtering Frenchmen and plundering French property.

Magna Carta, another direct product of the events of 1204, played its own, not entirely innocent, role in the debacle of 2016. Certainly, it was widely cited by the advocates of 'Brexit' as a totem of the English 'common law' supposedly set at odds with the Roman law traditions of continental Europe. The peddlers of this interpretation either deliberately ignored (or more likely remained profoundly ignorant of) the fact that Magna Carta emerged from a far wider European tradition of law. From its classical, civilian defence of 'res publica' and condemnation of judicial corruption, via its Augustinian committee of twenty-five barons, through to the materials it shares in common with the Statute of Pamiers and the reforming decrees of northern Spain, Magna Carta was not just an English but a thoroughly European response to political crisis. Roman jurisprudence, the Judaic Old Testament, Germanic tribal assemblies, French feudalism and papal

---

[30] For the effects upon Normandy, see A. J. Davis, *The Holy Bureaucrat: Eudes Rigaud and Religious Reform in Thirteenth-Century Normandy* (Ithaca, N.Y., 2006), pp. 94–6.

canon law all played a part in its making. Eight hundred years after it was first issued, Magna Carta remains both a highly charged and a potentially deceptive document.

In so far as the rebellion of 1215 and the making of Magna Carta have lessons to teach us, they suggest that the personal failings of a particular ruler (King John) or his entourage (the French-born constables and mercenaries of Magna Carta clauses 50–1) can undermine even the most ruthless of governmental systems. Without compromise and the careful management of the body politic, clashes between the ambitions of individual rulers and the will of an elite oligarchy (the barons) can lead to crisis and civil war. Yet from such clashes can emerge not only political turmoil, but in the case of Magna Carta, an insistence upon the rule of law, and (from this, albeit only after many further crises) a system of constitutional balance that fosters stability rather than chaos. Certainly, in 2017, as in 1215, 1715, 1815 or 1915, Great Britain seems to have lost none of its flair for constitutional crisis. In 2017, as in 1215, it is to be hoped, such crisis will foster constitutional innovation and the reinvention of the body politic. In 2017, as in 1215, the new, as ever, remains firmly rooted in the old.

4. The Church and Magna Carta in the thirteenth century

S. T. Ambler

The period of fifty years between the first issue of Magna Carta in 1215 and the confirmation of its authoritative version (1225) at Simon de Montfort's celebrated parliament of 1265 is heralded in Britain today as a critical stage in the emergence of the parliamentary state, when the limitation of royal power and the constriction of the king's ability to raise money through his feudal rights encouraged the strengthening of representative assemblies. Churchmen played leading parts in this story, though this is something that has generally gone unrecognized, perhaps for two reasons. First, academic research has for the most part focused on the role of laymen – whether barons, knights or even peasants – in the politics of this era. Second, the public perception of the age's central episodes, from the meeting on the meadow of Runnymede in 1215 to the Westminster parliament of 1265 oft-hailed as the 'first house of commons', views them as steps towards the modern system of democracy so cherished in the West, a polity seen today as antithetical to theocratic systems of government.[1] Yet research over the past four decades, and discoveries made in the last couple of years, suggest that this image of thirteenth-century English politics needs to be recast.

That churchmen, especially England's bishops, deserve a prominent place in the telling of this period's history was suggested in 1970, when John Baldwin published *Masters, Princes and Merchants*. This pathfinding study demonstrated how theologians of the Paris schools in the late twelfth century were deeply interested in what we might call moral philosophy and political ethics.[2] Using events described in the Bible, as well as scenarios from the world around them, the Paris scholars discussed the rights and wrongs of various difficult situations, in order to determine the morally justifiable course of action. Many of the matters discussed related to the highest echelons of society, considering how bishops, barons and knights

---

[1] For the 1265 parliament, see S. T. Ambler, 'Magna Carta: its confirmation at Simon de Montfort's parliament of 1265', *Eng. Hist. Rev.*, cxxx (2015), 801–30.

[2] *Masters, Princes and Merchants: the Social Views of Peter the Chanter and his Circle* (2 vols., Princeton, N.J., 1970).

S.T. Ambler, 'The Church and Magna Carta in the thirteenth century', in *Magna Carta: history, context and influence*, ed. L. Goldman (2018), pp. 41–50.

should interact with their kings. For instance: if the king has ordered his executioner to execute a subject, but the executioner knows that the man is innocent, should he proceed to carry out the sentence? If a king has ordered a knight to go to war, but the knight knows that the war is not justified, should he obey the order? One of the important scholars of Paris, the Englishman Stephen Langton, insisted that a king's decision to go against a subject or to prosecute a war must be approved by the judgement of a court.[3] The word 'court' in this context had two overlapping meanings: those prelates and magnates around the king and who offered him counsel, and the panel comprising the same group empowered to pronounce judgement upon one of its members accused of a fault. Both counselling the king and pronouncing a tenant-in-chief guilty or innocent meant providing 'judgement' for a royal decision. A king was expected not to act without first securing such judgement, or at least not without good reason or habitually, and indeed this was a profound expectation of medieval lordship more broadly. From this perspective Langton's assertion was not controversial, though it is important to note that he was coming at the problem from a theological perspective.

Baldwin's work was extended by the research of Philippe Buc, who published *L'ambiguïté du Livre* in 1994.[4] Here, Buc showed (among other things) that the Paris scholars held a deeply distrustful view of kingship as an institution. This was based upon the biblical origins of royal government, as identified by the Paris scholars: Cain's building of the first city (Genesis IV: 17), the construction of the tower by Nimrod (Genesis X–XI) and the Israelites' rejection of the rule of judges and demand for a king (I Kings VIII).[5] The last of these was particularly significant. The Israelites, having rejected God's direct rule, had demanded that God appoint a king to rule them. And so God sent his prophet, Samuel, with a warning about what the Israelites could expect from such a ruler:

> This will be the right of the king, that shall reign over you: He will take your sons, and put them in his chariots, and will make them his horsemen, and his running footmen to run before his chariots, And he will appoint of them to be his tribunes, and centurions, and to plough his fields, and to reap his corn, and to make him arms and chariots. Your daughters also he will take to make him ointments, and to be his cooks, and bakers. And he will take your fields, and your vineyards, and your best oliveyards, and give them to his

[3] J. Baldwin, 'Master Stephen Langton, future archbishop of Canterbury: the Paris schools and Magna Carta', *Eng. Hist. Rev.*, cxxiii (2008), 811–46, at pp. 815–20.

[4] P. Buc, *L'ambiguïté du Livre: prince, pouvoir, et peuple dans les commentaires de la Bible au Moyen Âge* (Paris, 1994).

[5] Buc, *L'ambiguïté du Livre*, pp. 237, 246–8.

servants. Moreover he will take the tenth of your corn, and of the revenues of your vineyards, to give his eunuchs and servants. Your servants also and handmaids, and your goodliest young men, and your asses he will take away, and put them to his work. Your flocks also he will tithe, and you shall be his servants. And you shall cry out in that day from the face of the king, whom you have chosen to yourselves. And the Lord will not hear you in that day, because you desired unto yourselves a king.[6]

This account invited two conclusions. First, God had never decreed kingship to be his chosen system of government. Kingship was conceived by humankind, in the course of rebellion against God. The Paris scholars connected this conclusion to the words of St. Paul, which foretold the end of days, when God would abolish the office of kingship: 'Afterwards the end, when he shall have delivered up the kingdom to God and the Father, when he shall have brought to nought all principality, and power'.[7] The second conclusion centred upon the *ius regis*, the 'right of the king' proclaimed by Samuel in his warning to the Israelites. Samuel was not setting out the rights to which a king was naturally entitled but, rather, describing kingship essentially as a series of crimes, an array of abuses that resulted from a weak and sinful mortal being placed in a position of authority over his fellows.[8]

The findings of Baldwin and Buc serve as important correctives to the entrenched conception of medieval political history, which held that politics was an essentially secular business. This view was epitomized by Sir James Holt, the pre-eminent Magna Carta scholar of his generation. In a chapter of his magnum opus *Magna Carta* (first published in 1965), 'The quality of the Great Charter', Holt argued strongly that Stephen Langton (appointed archbishop of Canterbury 1207, and present at the Runnymede negotiations in 1215) played no real part in the Charter's creation, except as a mere negotiator. Holt's argument was founded upon the assertion that Langton did not think it was the business of churchmen to intervene in 'secular' affairs. Although when Holt came to revise his *Magna Carta* for its second edition in 1992 it was now clear, as a result of Baldwin's research, that Stephen Langton nourished a deep interest in politics, based on his theological view of the world and his responsibilities within it, Holt did not change his views.[9] The prodigious influence that Holt's work enjoyed in the field of Magna Carta scholarship for decades perhaps explains why the topic of political theology was not incorporated into mainstream Magna Carta scholarship for some time.

---

[6] I Samuel VIII: 11–18.
[7] 1 Corinthians XV: 24; Buc, *L'ambiguïté du Livre*, pp. 123–70.
[8] Buc, *L'ambiguïté du Livre*, p. 248.
[9] J. C. Holt, *Magna Carta* (2nd edn., Cambridge, 1992), pp. 281, 284–9.

In recent years, there has been a resurgence in the debate about Langton's role in the creation of the first issue of the Charter in 1215.[10] Clearly, it was Langton who in 1215 brokered peace, bringing king and barons together at Runnymede. The chronicler Ralph of Coggeshall describes how, while King John and his men remained in their pavilions and the barons in their tents, the archbishop and his colleagues shuttled back and forth between them to negotiate a settlement.[11] To describe their role here with such a meagre term as 'go-between' would be a failure to grasp its nature. Bringing together two sides so divided by ideals and by enmity, and keeping them together long enough to hammer out a peace treaty, required true grit. It also required a profound authority, drawn from the charisma of the episcopal office and from the trust of both king and barons. As to the question of whether Langton authored particular clauses of the Charter, this is, in most cases, contentious. In an article of 2008, John Baldwin argued that Langton's commitment to the 'judgement by court' principle propelled him into rebellion between 1213 and 1215.[12] The implication was that Langton's agency was behind the Charter's headline chapter (thirty-nine of the 1215 issue): 'No free person is to be arrested, or imprisoned, or disseised, or outlawed, or exiled, or in any other way destroyed, nor will we go against him or send against him, except by the lawful judgment of his peers or by the law of the land.' This view has been rejected by David Carpenter (in an article of 2011), though Carpenter argued persuasively, based on a careful comparison of the 1215 Charter and the Articles of the Barons (a draft from which discussions at Runnymede proceeded), that Langton was responsible for inserting chapter one of the Charter, guaranteeing the freedom of the Church.[13] As far as most chapters are concerned, however, attempting to find a single 'author' would be a futile task: the Charter was a product of committee discussions and negotiations.

---

[10] For the part attributed to Langton in the making of Magna Carta during the 'rediscovery' of the archbishop from the 17th to the 19th centuries, see N. Vincent, 'Stephen Langton, archbishop of Canterbury', in *Etienne Langton, prédicateur, bibliste, théologien*, ed. L.-J. Bataillon, N. Bériou, G. Dahan, R. Quinto (Turnhout, 2010), pp. 51–123, at pp. 51–5, and a summary of more recent debate at pp. 92–3, with Vincent's contribution at pp. 93–7; for a bibliographic summary of recent debate, see D. A. Carpenter, 'Archbishop Langton and Magna Carta: his contribution, his doubts and his hypocrisy', *Eng. Hist. Rev.*, cxxvi (2011), 1041–65, at p. 1041 n.1, with Carpenter's contribution at pp. 1042–52.

[11] *Radulphi de Coggeshall Chronicon Anglicanum*, ed. J. Stevenson (Rolls Ser., 1875), p. 172.

[12] Baldwin, 'Master Stephen Langton', pp. 827–30. Baldwin's *Masters, Princes and Merchants* portrays a more conservative thinker, but the Langton of Baldwin's 2008 article is something of a radical.

[13] Carpenter, 'Archbishop Langton and Magna Carta', *in extenso*.

It is now possible, however, to say much more about the role of Langton and his suffragans in securing the Charter's issue in 1215, thanks to research conducted in the build-up to Magna Carta's anniversary celebrations in 2015 by the Magna Carta Project.[14] Extensive analysis of the documents issued by King John's chancery, and of the charters issued by the households of the bishops, was conducted by David Carpenter, Nicholas Vincent and Teresa Webber. The scribal hands from hundreds of charters were compared to the hands that produced the four surviving engrossments of the 1215 Charter. It now seems clear that at least two of the four, those kept at the cathedrals of Salisbury and Lincoln, were not written by royal scribes (as one would expect royal charters to be). Instead, they were written by scribes of the bishops' households. This research reveals, therefore, that the bishops provided their own scribes to help draw up engrossments of the Charter, in order to ensure that the contents of Magna Carta would be published above the wishes of a reluctant King John. Furthermore, the bishops were also the principal guardians of Magna Carta 1215, taking exemplars back to their cathedrals for safekeeping, from where they could be read or publicized.[15] Thus, in a phrase recently coined, the Church was central to the production, preservation and proclamation of the first issue of Magna Carta.

As time wore on, the interest of the English bishops in Magna Carta only increased. This was first revealed in 1998, when David d'Avray published a seminal article on Langton's political theology that engaged directly with the work of historians of English politics. D'Avray pointed to the central place of the bishops in the enforcement of Magna Carta in the thirteenth century. When a new version of the Charter was issued by Henry III's minority government in 1216, the controversial 'security for peace', which empowered twenty-five barons to 'distrain and afflict' the king in order to compel him to keep the Charter's terms, was removed, leaving Magna Carta with no means of enforcement.[16] This changed in 1225 when Stephen Langton, archbishop of Canterbury, and his suffragans stepped in to pronounce a general sentence of excommunication against all who would violate Magna Carta or the Charter of the Forest. The archbishop's actions were informed by his own biblical scholarship (found in his exegesis of Deuteronomy),

---

[14] The Project's website can be found at <http://magnacartaresearch.org>.

[15] N. Vincent and D. A. Carpenter, 'Feature of the month: June 2015 – Who did (and did not) write Magna Carta', *The Magna Carta Project* <http://magnacartaresearch.org/read/feature_of_the_month/Jun_2015_3> [accessed 11 Jan. 2016]; D. A. Carpenter, *Magna Carta* (2015), pp. 373–79.

[16] For the 'security of peace', see 'The 1215 Magna Carta: suffix A', *The Magna Carta Project*, trans. H. Summerson et al. <http://magnacartaresearch.org/read/magna_carta_1215/Suffix_A> [accessed 11 Jan. 2016].

which set out the need for kings to keep and abide by a written volume of the law and placed upon the shoulders of the clergy the responsibility for ensuring that this condition was met. Crucially, then, Langton had the opportunity as archbishop of Canterbury to put his thinking into practice. In acting thus, Langton set a precedent for his successors, encouraging a culture in which bishops were duty-bound to oversee royal government and to keep the king's rule within the law.[17] The confirmations of the 1225 Charter made throughout the course of Henry III's reign, and during the reign of his son Edward I, were likewise buttressed by a sentence of excommunication pronounced by England's bishops.

Descriptions of this sentence of excommunication (provided by the chronicler Matthew Paris) reveal the centrality of the bishops in the political culture of the Magna Carta era. In the course of a great assembly in 1237, the ritual was enacted in St. Katherine's chapel of Westminster Abbey. There the king stood, surrounded by his barons and bishops, with the bishops holding lighted candles. The king held his right hand on the Gospels and clutched a candle in his left, and delivered his oath to the archbishop of Canterbury, binding himself to uphold the Charters. All then uttered 'let it be done' to consummate the sentence, and the bishops turned over their candles onto the floor to extinguish them. This filled the room with smoke and the stench of the smoking wicks, which irritated the eyes and nostrils of those present. Now the archbishop proclaimed: 'thus may the condemned souls of those who violate the Charter be extinguished, and thus may they smoke and stink.'[18] This was a vivid and dramatic ritual, intended to imprint the sentence upon the memory by awakening the senses of sight, hearing, and smell. It summoned its participants to fulfil the communal responsibility of upholding the Charters and warned them of the spiritual danger of breaking their terms.

The duty to enforce Magna Carta was one that the bishops took seriously. In 1234, when Henry III had for a time cast off the principles of Magna Carta, Stephen Langton's pupil and successor as primate, Edmund of Abingdon, and his suffragans confronted the king in parliament with a catalogue of royal misdeeds and threatened to excommunicate him unless he mended his ways. It was a threat that the king took to heart, for he repented of his unjust actions and bent to Edmund's counsel (discussed

---

[17] D. L. d'Avray, '"Magna Carta": its background in Stephen Langton's academic biblical exegesis and its episcopal reception', *Studi Medievali*, 3rd ser., xxxvii (1998), 423–38.

[18] According to Matthew Paris, Henry held a candle for the ceremony of 1237 but refused to do so in 1253, on the grounds that he was not a priest (*Matthaei Parisiensis, Monachi Sancti Albani, Chronica Majora*, ed. H. R. Luard (7 vols., Rolls Ser., 1872–83) [hereafter *CM*], iii. 382, and v. 360–61 (for events of 1237); v. 377 (for 1253)).

below). On another occasion, three years later, the king and a number of his barons sought absolution from the archbishop, in case they had fallen under the sentence.[19]

As the thirteenth century continued, the bishops made increasing efforts to publicize the sentence of excommunication to the wider kingdom. As recent work by Felicity Hill has argued, they were driven by their responsibility to ensure good government but also by their pastoral obligations: if anybody violated Magna Carta, their soul would be placed in jeopardy, meaning that the bishops were duty-bound to warn their flocks of the Charter's terms, lest anybody fall under the sentence in ignorance.[20] The consequence was that Magna Carta was brought to a broad public, to parish churches as well as shire courts, and thus to the unfree as to the free, to women as well as men. The bishops, then, were instrumental in the expansion of the political community in the thirteenth century.

English bishops were able to act in this way because they were peculiarly powerful in respect to their king, and uniquely qualified to confront illegal royal actions. When the king acted illegally, refusing to follow due process or to consult his magnates and prelates, and provoked his barons to rebellion, the bishops could intervene. They possessed the ritual power to chastise him, purge him of his faults, and recreate him anew as king.[21] This can be seen in 1213: before Winchester Cathedral, the sin-ridden King John threw himself tearfully at the bishops' feet, begging their forgiveness for the faults he had committed against Church and kingdom. The bishops lifted him from the ground and led him into the cathedral, where John swore to defend the Church and her clergy, to maintain the good laws of his kingdom and to provide justice: effectively a renewal of his coronation oath.[22] The bishops' authority can be seen again in 1234. Between 1232 and 1233, under the malign influence of certain royal ministers, Henry III gave orders *per voluntatem regis* (acting according to his will and without judgement). This was a violation of the tenets of his office, as laid out by custom and guaranteed by Magna Carta, and provoked certain of his barons to rebellion. In response, Edmund of Abingdon, Stephen Langton's pupil and now archbishop of Canterbury, intervened. Edmund and his suffragans

---

[19] *The Letters of Robert Grosseteste, Bishop of Lincoln*, trans. F. A. C. Mantello and J. Goering (Toronto, 2010), pp. 252–4.

[20] F. Hill, 'Magna Carta, canon law and pastoral care: excommunication and the Church's publication of the charter', *Hist. Research*, lxxxix (2016), 636–50.

[21] S. T. Ambler, *Bishops in the Political Community of England, 1213–1272* (Oxford, 2017), pp. 61–81.

[22] Roger of Wendover, *Chronica, sive Flores Historiarum*, ed. H. O. Coxe (4 vols., 1842), iii. 260–61.

stood before the king and reproved Henry for the unjust treatment of his subjects, and warned him to desist or face the penalty of ecclesiastical censure. The king's response was humble and penitent, and he went on to rectify the wrongs he had committed.[23]

The role of the bishops here was ultimately founded upon the example of the Old Testament prophets, who were held to be the forerunners of the Christian clergy. First, the bishops drew authority from their role as anointers of kings. The place of the bishops in royal inauguration rites was founded upon Old Testament descriptions of the anointing of the kings of Israel by prophets,[24] and had been established since at least the mid tenth century in much of western Europe.[25] In England, bishops had long been central to the coronation ritual: they administered the coronation oath, anointed the candidate, and delivered a sermon on his duties as ruler.[26] In England, this crowning and anointing by prelates became essential to the monarch's authority.[27] This was not the case in many other European polities in the central middle ages, where kings were not generally anointed. The fact of the royal anointing was important to episcopal authority because, like baptism, it renewed the candidate and implied that those conferring the anointing had the right to correct him.[28]

Second, the bishops drew authority from the example of their Old Testament antecessors by looking to instances when God had sent his prophets to reprimand the wayward monarchs who oppressed the Israelites. The duty to reprimand erring kings in this manner had long been borne by English prelates: Björn Weiler has traced it through the centuries, from

[23] Wendover, iv. 294–7.

[24] I Samuel X: 1; I Samuel XVI: 13; I Kings I: 39; I Kings XIX: 15–16; II Kings IX: 6; J. L. Nelson, 'The lord's anointed and the people's choice: Carolingian royal ritual', in her *The Frankish World, 750–900* (1996), pp. 99–132, at p. 108.

[25] J. L. Nelson, 'Inauguration rituals', in her *Politics and Ritual in Early Medieval Europe* (1986), pp. 283–307, at 287.

[26] P. Stafford, 'The laws of Cnut and the history of Anglo-Saxon royal promises', *Anglo-Saxon England*, x (1982), 173–90, at pp. 185–6.

[27] English rulers since the Conquest were not considered king until crowned and anointed in Westminster Abbey. This custom continued until 1272, when necessity dictated that custom be broken (M. Morris, *A Great and Terrible King: Edward I and the Forging of Britain* (2008), pp. 103–4).

[28] J. L. Nelson, 'National synods, kingship as office, and royal anointing: an early medieval syndrome', in *Studies in Church History*, vii, ed. G. J. Cuming and D. Baker (Cambridge, 1971), 41–59, at pp. 52–3; Nelson, 'National synods', pp. 54–5. For the longer background of *admonitio*, see M. Suchan, 'Monition and advice as elements of politics', in *Patterns of Episcopal Power: Bishops in 10th and 11th Century Western Europe*, ed. L. Körntgen and D. Waßenhoven (2011), pp. 39–50; Stafford, 'Anglo-Saxon royal promises', *Anglo-Saxon England*, p. 188.

the Anglo-Saxon period up to the archiepiscopate of Stephen Langton (1207–26).[29] The most famous example, of course, was Thomas Becket, whose conflict with Henry II led to Becket's martyrdom at the hands of Henry's men in 1170. English bishops of the thirteenth century could thus draw on the authority not only of the Old Testament prophets but also of their predecessors when they reprimanded kings, and especially from the sanctified example of Becket (he was canonized in 1173), whose memory became talismanic.[30] Something changed in the thirteenth century, however: the manner of issue contested by the bishops. Where earlier prelates had chastised kings for their moral failings or defended the liberty of the Church, Langton and his successors chastised the king for offences against his people and defended the kingdom as a whole, in the interests of the broader community.[31] It was Langton, with his scholarly interest in political ethics, who was responsible for extending this duty.

These pools of authority combined to qualify the English bishops for the oversight of royal power, a duty and a right amplified by Stephen Langton's biblical scholarship, which argued that it was the responsibility of the priesthood to provide the king with written law. The strength of the episcopate in acting thus was enlivened by a forceful sense of corporate solidarity, developed through the thirteenth century as senior churchmen met frequently both in synods and regnal assemblies, where the king's frequent demands for taxation encouraged the prelates to engage with royal policy and to act collectively in resisting it.[32] This power of the English bishops to reform royal rule was unusual, in comparison with their colleagues in other European polities. For instance, the kingdoms of the Iberian Peninsula can be viewed as parallels to England, in that representative institutions similar to the English parliament emerged during the thirteenth century, wherein a penurious king was forced to bargain with his subjects. Yet, in the Iberian Peninsula, bishops had no power to oversee royal rule or correct the abuses of their kings, because they had no liturgical role in king-making, because they did not enjoy (or rather were not permitted to develop) the same sense of corporate solidarity, and because they were kept under the royal heel.[33] What was peculiar about the English experience, then, was the prominent place of religious leaders in the development of the parliamentary institution.

---

[29] B. K. Weiler, 'Bishops and kings in England, c.1066–1215', in *Religion and Politics in the Middle Ages: Germany and England by Comparison*, ed. L. Körntgen and D. Waßenhoven (Berlin, 2013), pp. 157–203.

[30] Ambler, *Bishops in the Political Community*, pp. 20–1, 64, 67–8, 96, 97–8, 117–18, 132–3.

[31] Ambler, *Bishops in the Political Community*, pp. 63–4.

[32] Ambler, *Bishops in the Political Community*, pp. 82–104.

[33] Ambler, *Bishops in the Political Community*, pp. 54, 99–103, 206.

The creation of Magna Carta and its entrenchment in political society were, therefore, intertwined with the strengthening of England's episcopate. Research over the past few decades has shown that regnal politics in this period was inherently religious, and that it became more and not less so even as the bureaucracy of the English State (so often seen as antithetical to charismatic politics) expanded, and as the parliamentary State emerged. Indeed, central to the political culture that produced the parliamentary State was the wielding of spiritual power by certain of its agents, and the understanding that spiritual and charismatic authority was as important in constraining the operation of kingship as the ability of barons and knights to refuse grants of taxation. The two, indeed, went hand in hand, since grants of taxation (made by assemblies of prelates, magnates and knights) were made only on condition that the king uphold the Charters, requiring the political community to participate in sentences of excommunication and subjecting them to its spiritual penalties. Contrary to the myths that have come to surround Magna Carta over the centuries, this world was not democratic, but theocratic.

5. Sir Edward Coke's resurrection of Magna Carta

George Garnett

On 28 April 1628 Sir Benjamin Rudyerd, M.P. for Downton, Wiltshire, told the house of commons:

> I shall be very glad to see that good, old decrepit Law of Magna Charta which hath been so long kept in, and lain bed-rid, as it were, I shall be glad I say to see it walk abroad again, with new Vigour and Lustre, attended by the Six Statutes; For questionless, it will be a general heartening to all the people.[1]

Rudyerd was contributing to the parliamentary debates provoked by King Charles I's arbitrary arrest and imprisonment of several individuals who had refused to subscribe to the forced loan which the king had attempted to exact, without parliamentary sanction, from certain of his subjects in 1627. To be precise, Rudyerd was urging the king's opponents in the house of commons to accept a compromise. The king had offered to confirm Magna Carta along with the six supplementary statutes passed by parliaments during the reign of Edward III, between 1328 and 1368. These statutes had both amplified and readjusted Magna Carta to the changed circumstances of the fourteenth century.[2] But the king would confirm these ancient bits of legislation only if his opponents sought no further, new restrictions on his exercise of his prerogative.

How had it come about that King Charles in 1628 sought to placate parliamentary opposition by offering a confirmation of Magna Carta, a royal document of the early thirteenth century, and its various fourteenth-century statutory elaborations and redefinitions? No English king had proposed defusing opposition in this way since Henry V in 1422, over two centuries before. And why were Magna Carta and the subsequent statutes suddenly being resurrected, Lazarus-like, from the sickbed to which Sir Benjamin

---

[1] *Commons Debates 1628*, ed. R. C. Johnson et al. (4 vols., 1977–97), iii. 128.

[2] F. Thompson, *Magna Carta: its Role in the Making of the English Constitution 1300–1629* (Minneapolis, Minn., 1948), pp. 9–32; J. C. Holt, 'The ancient constitution in medieval England', in *The Roots of Liberty: Magna Carta, Ancient Constitution, and the Anglo-American Tradition of the Rule of Law*, ed. E. Sandoz (1993), pp. 22–56.

G. Garnett, 'Sir Edward Coke's resurrection of Magna Carta', in *Magna Carta: history, context and influence*, ed. L. Goldman (2018), pp. 51–60.

Rudyerd thought the Charter had been confined for several centuries?[3] The answers to these questions are neither simple nor obvious, but they are best approached through the works of Sir Edward Coke, sometime chief justice of the king's bench and by 1628 incontrovertibly the principal legal mind in the parliamentary opposition to Charles.

Rudyerd's account of Magna Carta's antecedent moribundity was exaggerated. Sir John Baker has just published an enormous edition of readings on selected chapters of Magna Carta dating from the fifteenth and sixteenth centuries, the very period during which, according to Rudyerd, it had been bed-ridden.[4] Readings were the educational lectures on statutory texts delivered in the Inns of Court to law students. These particular readings reveal that Magna Carta – Henry III's reissue of Magna Carta of 1225, that is, which had ever since the thirteenth century been treated as the authoritative text – continued throughout those centuries to be a subject of considerable jurisprudential interest, despite its increasing obsolescence in practical terms.

That interest is hardly surprising, given that the Magna Carta of 1225 was the first item in the English statute book. Magna Carta was the foundational statute, as it were. It would therefore have been well known to all law students, even the most elementary or indolent. It is difficult to generalize, but the readings from this period suggest that Magna Carta was used by law lecturers in the Inns of Court mainly as a very familiar hook on which to hang explorations of instructive legal problems. Sometimes these were framed in terms of real cases, excavated from the Year Books, the records of interlocutory proceedings in court. Sometimes the cases were hypothetical, manufactured by the lecturer in order to raise some interesting legal conundrum. The readings ostensibly based on Magna Carta therefore in practice strayed a very long way from the first document in the statute book as they explored those problems. A chapter of Magna Carta did no more than provide the starting point. Or as Coke put it of recent law readings in general, they were 'long, obscure, and intricate, full of new conceits, liker rather to riddles than lectures, which when they are opened they vanish away like smoake, and the readers are like lapwings, who seem to be nearest their nests, when they are farthest from them'.[5] As this disparaging characterization suggests, Coke rejected such recent illusory and distracting elaborations, and presented himself as returning to the essentials of the text itself.

[3] G. Garnett, 'Magna Carta through eight centuries', *Oxford Dictionary of National Biography* (2015) <https://doi.org/10.1093/ref:odnb/107251> [accessed 22 March 2018].

[4] *Selected Readings and Commentaries on Magna Carta 1400–1604*, ed. J. H. Baker (Selden Society, cxxxii, 2015).

[5] Edward Coke, *I Institutes*, fo. 280a–b.

By the time he published this criticism of the practices of modern law lecturers, in his *First Institutes* (1628), Coke had developed what was for centuries and in many respects still remains the most influential assessment of English legal history. For reasons explored elsewhere, he presented the fourteenth and fifteenth centuries – the period of the Year Books, and of Thomas Littleton, whose great work on land law was the subject of Coke's *First Institutes* – as English law's golden age. In that period, he erroneously asserted, readings had still been cited frequently in court proceedings, because, by inference, they were then still of use to legal practitioners. They had not yet degenerated into the deceptively irrelevant academic exercises of recent times, which were of no use at all to lawyers engaged in court proceedings, the context in which Coke considered English law was most effectively formulated. He presented himself, as mentioned earlier, as restoring or purifying the currently debased law. But his interpretation of English legal history had been fully formed long before he wrote, in 1628, this disparaging comment about modern readings. He had begun to sketch his interpretation in the readings that he himself wrote during Elizabeth I's reign. He had greatly elaborated them in his artful prefatory essays to the volumes of his *Reports*, which he started to publish in 1600.[6]

The *Reports* printed what he presented as transcripts of jurisprudentially key court cases from the preceding forty years. They were intended as a definitive substitute for the now defunct sequence of Year Books, which had expired (for reasons Coke never addressed) by the mid sixteenth century. His first elaborate preface is that to the *Third Reports*, published in 1602, and the last to the *Tenth Reports*, published in 1614. These prefaces develop an account of English law as both immemorial and continuous. They were written in an engaging English prose, their style of reasoning is artfully whimsical, and they require little legal knowledge on the part of readers. They were, in other words, intended for a wide, lay as well as a legally learned, audience. Their account of the history of English law was intended to shore up that law, and therefore the liberties which were considered to be grounded in it, first against James I's early threats of Union between his English and Scottish kingdoms, including a Union of the respective legal systems of those two kingdoms. The consequence of such a legal Union was widely accepted to be the abolition of English common law, and the liberties that English law was deemed to embody. Second, and more broadly, even as the threat of Union between England and Scotland receded, Coke was seeking to forestall the new king's various devious attempts to sidestep parliament.

---

[6] This is a summary of the argument of G. Garnett, '"The ould fields": law and history in the Prefaces to Sir Edward Coke's *Reports*', *Jour. Legal History*, xxxiv (2013), 245–84.

In the preface to *Eighth Reports*, published in 1611, Coke presented the Magna Carta of 1225 as the first surviving written summary of English law in statutory form. There was nothing novel or unconventional about this. It was in accord with English legal tradition reaching back to the late thirteenth century; but Coke here greatly elaborated it. He knew that Henry III's Charter was a confirmation of John's of 1215, the text of which he had not yet bothered to try to excavate, because that was not what was in the statute book; but he traced the tradition of the royal charter of liberties granted to the king's subjects back through Henry II's coronation charter in 1154, Stephen's coronation charter in 1135, and Henry I's coronation charter in 1100, to William the Conqueror. William the Conqueror had not issued a coronation charter, but, according to some thirteenth- and fourteenth-century chroniclers and a twelfth-century apocryphal law code which Coke accepted as authentic, the first Norman king had summoned an assembly of the English nobility which had summarized existing, indeed immemorial, English law, labelled as '*the lawes of King Edward*'. This label meant not that these laws were Edward the Confessor's own legislation; rather they were the existing English laws which Edward the Confessor had endorsed, and which William the Conqueror, in the wake of his conquest of England, was in turn confirming. These laws, compiled by an assembly of the nobility under William I, had been made 'into a *Magna Carta* (the ground-worke for all those that after followed)'.[7] Henry III's Charter of 1225 was simply the first extant statutory exemplification of that ancient, indeed immemorial English law, embodied after the Norman Conquest in successive Magnae Cartae, issued by successive kings. Coke first published this analysis in 1611, in the preface to *Eighth Reports*. But it was built on his much earlier, briefer sketches of English legal history, preserved in his extant readings written during Elizabeth I's reign, and amplified above all in the preface to *Third Reports* (1602) and the substantial report of Caudrey's Case which he had included in *Fifth Reports* (1605). Nevertheless, the central role in English legal history which he now attributed in print to Magna Carta was new to the preface of *Eighth Reports* of 1611.

This did not, however, constitute Coke's first detailed written consideration of Magna Carta. Already in Michaelmas Term 1604, Coke had inserted into one of his manuscript notebooks – the sources for all his *Reports* on individual court cases – a memorandum on Magna Carta chapter 29, that chapter of 1225 Magna Carta which elided chapters 39 and 40 of John's Charter of 1215.[8] This unprinted memorandum does not place Magna Carta

---

[7] Edward Coke, *Eighth Reports*, p. v.
[8] Baker, *Selected Readings*, pp. 394–402.

in an historical context, as Coke would do in the preface to *Eighth Reports*. Perhaps it does not do so because he had not yet in 1604 realized how Magna Carta could be made central to his history of English law, or perhaps just because the memorandum was addressed to legal professionals, rather than also to the wider, unlearned audience to the prefaces of his *Reports*. In it Coke drew a connection between this chapter of Magna Carta and that early Tudor invention, the writ *habeas corpus ad subjiciendum*, an order to 'produce the body ... to undergo [whatever our court should order]'.[9]

Originally, *habeas corpus* had been an expression of royal prerogative – an instruction in the name of the monarch to produce any prisoner, whoever currently held him in custody, in practice most often a royal councillor or one of the conciliar courts, themselves acting on the basis of the royal prerogative. Prerogative was thus used to trump prerogative, not in order to liberate a prisoner, but to bring him before the court issuing the writ – in the particular case of *habeas corpus ad subjiciendum*, the court of the king's bench. Yet because the writ specified that it had to be returned with the date and cause of detention, it afforded that court an opportunity also to review the justification for imprisonment, and therefore at least potentially to release the prisoner, to set him at liberty. By connecting the writ with this chapter of Magna Carta in his memorandum, Coke was transforming this mechanism for transferring a prisoner from the custody of some other agent of the king into the custody of the court of the king's bench. He was transforming it into a right of the king's subject to contest arbitrary imprisonment at the king's command. In Coke's view this Tudor innovation could provide the remedy for infringement of chapter 29 and the supplementary statutes which neither Magna Carta itself nor the statutes had provided. In other words, it defined the 'due process of law' to which those statutes had referred, although they had never spelled out what the term meant. Magna Carta had occasionally been invoked in the sixteenth century by those contesting their imprisonment,[10] but so far as I can establish Coke was the first lawyer to base *habeas corpus* on chapter 29 of Magna Carta. The move was prophetic, in the sense that he wrote this memorandum twenty-three years prior to the Five Knights' Case of 1627, in which *habeas corpus* would be treated by counsel for the imprisoned knights as the means for enforcing chapter 29 of Magna Carta, with the aim of assessing the legality of the king's actions according to what this

---

[9] P. D. Halliday, *Habeas Corpus, from England to Empire* (Cambridge, Mass., 2010), pp. 16–18; J. H. Baker, *An Introduction to English Legal History* (4th edn., Oxford 2002), pp. 146–7.

[10] J. H. Baker, 'Personal liberty under the common law 1200–1600', in his *Collected Papers on English Legal History* (3 vols., Cambridge, 2013), ii. 871–900, at pp. 893–9.

very chapter of Magna Carta termed 'the law of the land'.[11] In 1604 Coke was King James's attorney general, and his inventive use of *habeas corpus* in conjunction with Magna Carta and the fourteenth-century statutes on due process might be seen as a novel device to enable the common law judges, acting of course in the king's name, to keep certain prerogative jurisdictions in check – an objective which continued to remain close to Coke's heart.[12] But he had started publishing his *Reports* as attorney general under Queen Elizabeth. Her successor's behaviour as king had exacerbated, not allayed, the concern which Coke had already felt prior to 1603. In Coke's case, being a senior law officer did not necessarily make for deference to the royal will. Indeed, rather the contrary. In the memorandum he already in 1604 made grandiloquent claims which suggested that Magna Carta chapter 29 (and by implication the *habeas corpus* which he here connected with it) might have a much wider application: the chapter, he alleged, protected 'everything that anyone has in this world, or that concerns the freedom and liberty of his body or his freehold, or the benefit of the law to which he is inheritable, or his native country in which he was born, or the preservation of his reputation or goods, or his life, blood, and posterity'.[13] As such, moreover, it was 'merely a declaration of the old law of the land' – the law which had already been old at the time of Magna Carta, and which had been explicitly invoked in chapter 29.

That brief characterization – not in itself innovatory – might be interpreted as prompting Coke's later incorporation of Magna Carta into the scheme of English legal history which he had first outlined in any detail (but without any reference to Magna Carta) two years beforehand in the preface to *Third Reports*. In the terms of his later disparagement of recent readings in the Inns of Court, he was not a jurisprudential lapwing, farthest from his nest when he appeared closest to it; nor was he creating a smokescreen which obscured the real issue.[14] On the contrary, he had identified the foundation for property, liberty, and even life itself in this very chapter of the earliest extant English statute.

If Sir Benjamin Rudyerd had ever read Coke's memorandum, which seems unlikely – if it circulated at all, it did so in manuscript – he might have identified it as the point at which Magna Carta had begun to stir in its centuries-old sickbed. It is, however, highly likely that Sir Benjamin would have read the preface to *Eighth Reports*, not least because of the role that

---

[11] Thompson, *Magna Carta*, pp. 326–35; J. S. Hart Jr., *The Rule of Law, 1603–1660: Crowns, Courts and Judges* (Harlow, 2003), pp. 122–30.

[12] Baker, *Selected Readings*, pp. xc–xci.

[13] Baker, *Selected Readings*, p. 394.

[14] Above, p. 000.

Magna Carta came to play in political debate in 1628. In that year Magna Carta was central to the Petition of Right, the device adopted, at Coke's instigation, by the parliamentary opposition in order to circumscribe Charles I. In the Petition of Right Magna Carta was explicitly conjoined with *habeas corpus*, and the Five Knights' Case of the previous year was explicitly invoked.[15] To this Petition King Charles was eventually forced to give his grudging assent. It was the sort of measure he had sought to pre-empt by offering to confirm Magna Carta and the supplementary statutes, on condition that there was no further elaboration. The Petition was just the sort of elaboration he had sought to fend off.

Coke was famously dismissed as chief justice of the king's bench by James I in 1616. By that point he had published the last volume of *Reports* which he would see through the press. After his dismissal he was ordered to make many amendments to the published texts of the *Reports* – an order to which he responded as provocatively as one would expect of him.[16] He was already, however, at work on his new and even more ambitious jurisprudential project, his *Institutes*. His aim in the *Institutes* was to produce the most comprehensive written survey of English law ever, a replacement for (and by implication an improvement on) the great thirteenth-century law book known as *Bracton*, which still remained at that point the most comprehensive and detailed statement of English law in existence.

His choice of title for his new work was obviously an allusion to the sixth-century Roman emperor Justinian, whose *Institutes*, one of the four constituent parts of the *Corpus Iuris Civilis*, had also been presented as a legal text-book. Coke's *Institutes* bore more than a passing resemblance to the *Corpus Iuris Civilis* in another sense, but to the *Corpus* in the form it assumed in the later middle ages onwards, not to the sixth-century original: it consisted both of the texts of authoritative sources of law, and Coke's extensive glosses on them. However, in Coke's opinion the nature of his gloss was yet another manifestation of the superiority of English jurisprudence over Roman:

> their glosses and commentaries are written by doctors, which be advocates, and in a manner private interpretations; and our expositions or commentaries upon Magna Charta, and other statutes, are resolutions of judges in courts of justice in judiciall courses of proceeding, either related and reported in our books, or extant in judiciall records, or in both, and therefore being collected together, shall ... produce certainty.[17]

---

[15] Thompson, *Magna Carta*, pp. 335–9.
[16] Garnett, "'The ould fields'", pp. 282–3.
[17] Edward Coke, *The Second Part of the Institutes of the Lawes of England* (1642) (hereafter *Second Institutes*), 'A Proeme'.

Such certainty, based on law forensically defined by judges in public, was inconceivable in Roman jurisprudence, which by contrast with English was based on the private opinions of jurists and advocates. Coke proclaims it in the preface to *Second Institutes*, the volume which glossed at length certain statutes which Coke considered most significant, beginning, like the statute book, and as Coke underlined, with Magna Carta, and ending in the reign of James I.

The prefaces to all volumes of *Institutes* other than the *Second* are terse; the volume which follows the preface is allowed to speak for itself. Only that to *Second Institutes* is substantial and discursive, and in that sense comparable to the prefaces to the *Reports*. However, the only statute which this preface discusses explicitly is Magna Carta; the subsequent thirty-eight statutes included in the volume receive no explicit mention. Among the thirty-eight are included Edward I's *Confirmationes chartarum* of 1297 and his *Articuli super chartas* of 1300. Coke's gloss on Magna Carta, like his glosses throughout the first two parts of the *Institutes*, is designed for use by legal practitioners. Its focus is on the detailed interpretation of particular passages in the texts, by reference to records of forensic proceedings, primarily from the Year Books, and other sources which Coke regarded as authoritative. This format means that there is no opportunity to develop a sustained argument, even on the modest scale of the prefaces to the *Reports*. The focus is on particular textual detail. The preface to *Second Institutes* is therefore the most obvious occasion in the *Institutes* when Coke steps back from minute textual examination in order to draw wider lessons.

In it he repeated almost verbatim what he had said in that to *Eighth Reports*, which in turn echoes the memorandum of 1604: Magna Carta was 'for the most part declaratory of the principall grounds of the fundamentall laws of England, and for the residue it is additionall to supply some defects of the common law; and it was no new declaration'. He acknowledged, again, that King John had issued a Magna Carta in 1215, though Coke also admitted that John had attempted to wriggle out of it, by claiming that it had been issued under duress. That was not, however, true of Henry III's Magna Carta of 1225. By virtue of the authorities Coke cited, and the earlier royal legislation he invoked, he sought to demonstrate that insofar as the 1225 Magna Carta did not simply endorse then current common law, it reinstated what had recently been disregarded or contravened, by King John and King Richard, whose reigns had been 'troublesome and irregular times' during which 'divers oppressions, exactions, and injuries were incroached upon the subject in these kings names'. He established what ancient practice had been not by reference to court records – for there were none extant – but to late thirteenth and fourteenth-century books –

the *Modus tenendi parliamentum* and the *Mirror of Justices* – both of which affected to be pre-Conquest works, in the former case dating from the reign of Edward the Confessor, in the latter from that of King Arthur. Coke devotes most attention to chapter 29, the chapter which had been the main focus of his attention in the memorandum of 1604: 'as the goldfiner will not out of the dust, threds, or shreds of gold, let passe the least crum, in respect of the excellency of the metal: so ought not the learned reader to let passe any syllable of this law, in respect of the excellency of the matter.'[18] He attempts to establish a genealogy of cases in support of the connection he had drawn between the chapter and *habeas corpus*.

But the *Second Institutes* was not published during Coke's lifetime. James I had ordered an investigation into Coke's *Reports*, and Coke had thumbed his nose at the suggested revisions.[19] In 1621 several of Coke's books were confiscated – in 1628 he told the house of commons he would give £300 to get the most precious manuscripts back.[20] In that year he published his *First Institutes*, a massive gloss on Littleton's *Tenures,* and in the brief preface gave notice that he already had in hand a similar treatment of Magna Carta. In view of the political events of that year, he was clearly needling his sovereign; and successfully so. Coke's books and manuscripts were searched again in 1631, not long after Sir Robert Cotton had been barred from using his own library, because the material he was unearthing from his books was considered by the authorities to be too subversive. The king now ordered that every effort should be made to ensure that Coke's promised commentary on Magna Carta did not 'come forth'.[21] In 1634, as the resurrector of Magna Carta himself lay on his death-bed, the king's agents rifled through his books and papers in the study below. A trunk full of books and papers was dispatched to Charles in person, at Bagshot, '& there broken open by his Majesty'. Charles was evidently unwilling to trust anyone to do that job for him. Inside the box was a smaller trunk, which did indeed contain 'an exposicion upon Magna Carta and other ancient statutes'[22] – the draft of *Second Institutes* to which Coke had menacingly referred in the preface to *First Institutes*. In 1641 the house of commons voted that this, together with the drafts of *Third* and *Fourth Institutes*, should be released and published, and chose to do so on the very day of the earl of Strafford's execution.[23] That decision exemplified the shibbolethic

[18] *Second Institutes*, fo. 57a.
[19] Garnett, '"The ould fields"', p. 282.
[20] *Commons Debates 1628*, iii. 166.
[21] The National Archives of the U.K., SP 16/183, 18, fo. 29.
[22] London, Lambeth Palace Library, MS. 943, 371–2.
[23] Garnett, '"The ould fields"', p. 284.

status which Coke's commentary had achieved, for both the king and his opponents; it had, as Sir Benjamin Rudyerd had prophesied to the house of commons in 1628, become 'a general heartening to all the people'.

But Coke would have been horrified by the use to which his work would be put by the end of the 1640s. In *Behemoth*, Thomas Hobbes characterized the preliminary conflicts of the 1620s and 1630s thus: 'it were a Warre ... yet there was no bloodshed; they shot at one another nothing but paper'.[24] Coke never envisaged the shift from printed legal argument to firearms and, ultimately, to the axe wielded by the executioner of the king at the behest of what purported to be an English law court sitting in, of all places, that legal Holy of Holies, Westminster Hall. Nevertheless his historical elaboration of the traditional doctrine of English legal continuity, at the heart of which he came to place Magna Carta, ended up playing a very important part in fashioning the weapon with which the veil of the temple was rent in twain. It also, both before and after, became foundational to the liberty of the subject, not only in England, but throughout the English-speaking world, and eventually beyond.

[24] Thomas Hobbes, *Behemoth*, ed. P. Seaward (Oxford, 2010), pp. 251–2.

6. 'More precious in your esteem than it deserveth'? Magna Carta and seventeenth-century politics*

Rachel Foxley

Magna Carta was born in a time of conflict in the thirteenth century, when King John's overbearing rule was challenged by his barons. In the seventeenth century Magna Carta was drawn into another conflict between a king and his subjects: the English Civil War or English Revolution of the 1640s. King Charles I was not a tyrannical king in the way that King John was, but he was rather rigid in his approach to kingship, and he presided over three separate kingdoms (England, Scotland and Ireland) which were not easy to rule harmoniously, oversaw unpopular religious policies, and brought England into wars in the 1620s which placed a huge burden on the population. The resulting political tensions effectively brought about the breakdown of the English constitution. Under pressure from Scottish rebels, Charles called two English parliaments in 1640. His attempt to bolster his position in his largest kingdom backfired, as the Long Parliament which met in November 1640 exploited Charles's weak position to prolong its own life and challenge the king's unpopular counsellors and policies. In the autumn of 1641, rebellion broke out in Ireland as well. The king and the parliament both raised troops, but instead of sending them to suppress the Irish rising, they began a civil war in England. Parliament defeated the king in the English Civil Wars of 1642–6 and 1648. Charles was executed in 1649, and a failed experiment in republican government ensued before Charles II was able to reclaim his father's throne in 1660.

But the civil wars were not just fought on the battlefield. The warring sides fought through print and propaganda too: 'newsbooks', the newspapers of the day, established themselves in English life permanently in the 1640s, and pamphlets also poured from the presses. In these media a battle of ideas was fought, and it was able to reach a broader audience than had ever had access to printed political news before. Both sides appealed to ordinary readers to support their cause in the civil war, and they needed

* I am very grateful for the opportunity to speak at Peking University at the Anglo-Chinese Conference of Historians on Magna Carta in September 2015, and would like to thank all the organizers and hosts for their warm welcome, hospitality and discussion.

R. Foxley, '"More precious in your esteem than it deserveth"? Magna Carta and seventeenth-century politics', in *Magna Carta: history, context and influence*, ed. L. Goldman (2018),pp. 61–77.

justifications. Magna Carta was one of the authorities they called on in order to argue their case – both royalists and parliamentarians invoked its support for their preferred interpretations of the English constitution and the current conflict. These ways of appealing to a wide audience were put to a new use from 1646 when a group of radical parliamentarians – who later became known as the Levellers – started to propose a much more daring and innovative settlement for the kingdom than the parliamentarian leadership was prepared to countenance. The parliamentarians were a coalition – and a bitterly divided one. Most were still intent on restoring the king to the throne, albeit with conditions imposed on him. For them it was natural to invoke the 'ancient constitution', and the checks on royal power which measures such as Magna Carta embodied. The Levellers, by contrast, argued for a settlement based on a unicameral elected chamber exercizing the sovereignty of the people through its legislative power. This would be far from a return to the pre-civil-war status quo, and the Levellers' arguments were often based on abstract ideas of natural rights rather than historical or legal precedent. However, even the Levellers looked backwards to Magna Carta. In the second part of this paper I will ask why that was, but first I will set out the background to the civil war use of Magna Carta by looking at the political conflicts of the 1620s and the contribution of the great common lawyer Sir Edward Coke.

Sir Edward Coke and Magna Carta before the civil war

Magna Carta had not held a prominent place in the political debate of the sixteenth century. One of the things Magna Carta did – in fact the first thing it did – was guarantee the liberties of the English Church. In the sixteenth century this was rather inconvenient to Henry VIII and his protestant successors who wrested the Church away from Rome and asserted their own royal authority over it. For this reason, among others, Magna Carta was not particularly prominent in political debate in the sixteenth century – it was not something that Protestants wanted to dwell on. But in the early seventeenth century Magna Carta came to be totemic in politics, something that almost everyone at the very least paid lip service to.

After the death of Elizabeth I in 1603, she was succeeded by her cousin James VI of Scotland, who now became James I of England. There must have been a collective sigh of relief that the Virgin Queen's succession problem had been solved peacefully, in spite of her stubborn refusal to solve it herself. But having a Scottish king ruling England brought its own problems. James brought with him well-developed theories of royal power, and an outsider's perspective on the idiosyncratic English legal system, the common law, which was not used in Scotland. A highly educated man who fancied himself as a political theorist, James had committed his views on monarchy to print in the *Trew Law of Free Monarchies* and *Basilicon Doron*, which were republished for the benefit of his new English subjects in 1603. He upheld an ideal of good kingship: because kings were divinely anointed, they were accountable directly to God for the virtue and benevolence of their rule. But they were accountable *only* to God, as their power came only and directly from him. It was unclear whether kings were subject to the law – but the implication seemed to be that they *created* it rather than *obeyed* it. As James told his subjects much later in his reign in a rather more informal work – a manuscript 'libel' which he wrote and circulated in response to an attack on royal policies in the same medium – 'Kings doe make Lawes to bridle yow'.[1] Subjects wanting protection against the king might well appeal to Magna Carta, which seemed to them to guarantee that their laws, or at least their legal system, had independent status and were not at the mercy of the king. The lessons which James I himself drew from the story of Magna Carta were rather different:

> The Charter which yow great doe call
> Came first from Kings to stay your fall ...

James had been willing to admit in a 1610 speech to parliament that in 'settled kingdoms' subjects were protected by laws graciously granted by former kings. As his poem suggests, Magna Carta was one of these, but its 'overbold' promoters had been seeking their own greatness.[2] As Paul Christianson suggests, James may have made considerable efforts to come to terms with the common law tradition which was part of the kingdom he inherited in 1603. However, some of his words could be read differently, even if they were now in the past; and James was still bold enough to suggest reform to the common law. In addition, James had hoped to unite England and Scotland into a single kingdom – which again might pose a threat to England's legal system. A resurgence of interest in the distinctive character of England's customary system of common law was a natural response to the early years of his reign.[3]

---

[1] James I, 'The wiper of the people's tears' (late 1622/1623), a libel in response to a libel called 'The comons tears', line 114 <http://www.earlystuartlibels.net/htdocs/spanish_match_section/Nvi1.html> [accessed 12 Dec. 2016]

[2] James I, 'The wiper of the people's tears', lines 118–125.

[3] For a more detailed account of these issues, and James's changing positions, see P. Christianson, 'Ancient constitutions in the age of Sir Edward Coke and John Selden', in *The Roots of Liberty: Magna Carta, Ancient Constitution, and the Anglo-American Tradition of Rule of Law*, ed. E. Sandoz (Columbia and London, 1993), pp. 89–146.

However, it was in the reign of Charles I that Magna Carta took on even greater importance. Charles inherited the throne in 1625 and responded to popular pressure in entering into the military conflicts on the continent, going to war against Spain and also France. Parliaments were frequent in the 1620s, and Charles hoped to work harmoniously with them – he had sat in the house of lords as prince of Wales. However, the disastrous progress and financial burden of the wars exacerbated existing tensions instead of uniting the country. Historians no longer see the early seventeenth century as a 'high road to civil war': the vast amount of scholarship produced by revisionist historians including Conrad Russell and Kevin Sharpe subjected the view that the civil war formed part of an inevitable social and political process to sharp scrutiny, and demonstrated that civil war in England was far from inevitable.[4] However, post-revisionist historians challenged the revisionists' picture of a culture of consensus in early Stuart politics. It is now clear that pre-civil-war England, particularly in the 1620s, experienced political conflict which was more ideological and less contingent than revisionist historians were prepared to admit.[5]

War in Europe put huge pressures on the English state. The parliaments which were called in the 1620s, partly in order to vote money for English military efforts, were a forum for some of the political conflicts which resulted. In response to war and to criticism in parliament, the government took actions which seemed to its critics to overstep the boundaries of the royal prerogative. Could the king, for example, rightfully raise money without consent in parliament, as he attempted to do in the Forced Loan of 1626? This move was met by significant and increasingly orchestrated opposition, and the government responded punitively in some high-profile cases. The imprisonment of some non-payers without cause shown provoked the Five Knights' Case, which again raised difficult questions about the limits of the

---

[4] C. Russell, *Parliaments and English Politics, 1621–1629* (Oxford, 1979); C. Russell, *The Causes of the English Civil War* (Oxford, 1990); C. Russell, *The Fall of the British Monarchies 1637–1642* (Oxford, 1991); K. Sharpe, *The Personal Rule of Charles I* (New Haven, Conn., 1992).

[5] For an influential set of post-revisionist essays emphasizing conflict in pre-civil-war politics, see *Conflict in Early Stuart England: Studies in Religion and Politics 1603–1642*, ed. R. Cust and A. Hughes (Harlow, 1989). Further studies emphasizing the conflicts involved in politics, particularly in the parliaments of the 1620s, are R. Cust, *The Forced Loan and English Politics 1626–1628* (Oxford, 1987); T. Cogswell, *The Blessed Revolution: English Politics and the Coming of War* (Cambridge, 1989); L. J. Reeve, *Charles I and the Road to Personal Rule* (Cambridge, 1989). On conflicts of ideology as well as conflict in practical politics, see J. P. Sommerville, *Royalists and Patriots: Politics and Ideology in England 1603–1640* (1999), but contrast the revisionist view provided by G. Burgess, *The Politics of the Ancient Constitution: an Introduction to English Political Thought 1600–1642* (Basingstoke, 1992).

king's prerogative and gave those critical of the government cause to look back into English legal history for broader reassurances.

Magna Carta offered the members of parliament who were critical of these royal expedients one rhetorical tool that they could use as they tried to define, reinforce, or even tighten the limits of royal power. Magna Carta was useful for various reasons. It was a precedent for limits being placed on kings, had been confirmed by numerous monarchs, and had become the first statute included in collections of the laws of England – although the version which had become standard was that reissued in 1225 under Henry III, not the original 1215 version. The famous chapters on justice – in 1225 amalgamated into chapter 29 – offered protection against arbitrary imprisonment and other punishment without due process. In the context of the Five Knights' Case such a venerable precedent was welcome. The requirement of the original 1215 Magna Carta that 'No scutage or aid is to be imposed in our kingdom except by the common counsel of our kingdom' did not survive into the 1225 version, but the parliamentarians of the 1620s could cite Edward I's later statute 'De tallagio non concedendo' to the same effect. Taxes had to be approved in parliament, and these thirteenth-century laws confirmed it.

Sir Edward Coke was a leading figure in the political use of Magna Carta in the parliaments of the 1620s, and his interpretation of the charter was published after his death by the Long Parliament on the eve of the civil war. Coke exemplifies the way in which the English common law legal system (different from the Roman law system widely used in other parts of Europe and in Scotland) became central to politics in England. Coke was both an extremely eminent common lawyer, and an increasingly troublesome politician and member of parliament towards the end of his life in the 1620s.[6] His legal career was stellar: he had risen to be attorney general, chief justice of common pleas and then chief justice of king's bench. His influence on legal thought went far beyond his own practice, however, as he made large amounts of case-law accessible through his volumes of Reports, which also offered interpretations of English law and history. Coke's lengthy period of eminence was not untroubled: he was dismissed from the bench in 1616, and suspended from the privy council, but although he could be stubborn on points of principle, he was far from a consistent critic of the king. David Chan Smith has argued that in fact Coke saw the common law as working harmoniously with the royal prerogative, and believed that necessary legal

[6] For narrative analyses of Coke's career, see S. D. White, *Sir Edward Coke and the Grievances of the Commonwealth* (Manchester, 1979); A. D. Boyer, *Sir Edward Coke and the Elizabethan Age* (Stanford, Calif., 2003); D. Chan Smith, *Sir Edward Coke and the Reformation of the Laws: Religion, Politics and Jurisprudence, 1578–1616* (Cambridge, 2014).

reforms would serve to strengthen rather than weaken royal authority.[7] It was towards the end of his long career that Coke became a key critic of royal policy. He did not return to the judiciary after 1616, and became more prominent as a political than a judicial figure, particularly as an M.P. in the parliaments of the 1620s. His actions led to imprisonment in 1621–2 and to attempts – unsuccessful in 1624, successful in 1626 – to prevent him sitting in parliament.[8] However, he sat in most of the parliaments of the 1620s and his critique of royal policy – and use of Magna Carta in this cause – culminated in the creation of the Petition of Right in 1628.

Coke's thought has been given great prominence by some historians, particularly those who see the common law as providing a 'language' which structured political thought and discourse in early Stuart England. Coke was the archetypal example of the early Stuart 'common law mind' identified by J. G. A. Pocock, and also figures largely in Alan Cromartie's more recent argument for a 'constitutionalist revolution', based on common law, which led into the English Revolution of the mid century.[9] These interpretations see the politics of the early seventeenth century as framed by and often argued through the language and resources of the common law tradition, and Coke as a key lawyer-politician takes on a prominent role in such arguments. Coke's vision was of an 'ancient constitution' framed by the continuous practice of the common law, and ultimately bounded only by the reason inherent in that law. The common law, in Coke's view, was competent to adjudicate on the powers of government and set limits to the king's prerogative.[10] For Coke the ancient constitution, the common law, and even parliament, stretched back before the Norman Conquest; and since the Conquest, kings had sworn to obey the laws. Kingship thus existed within the framework of common law, rather than pre-existing or presiding over it. This made the law a crucially important political tool, especially in the hands of an apparently authoritative interpreter, such as Coke in the

[7] Chan Smith, *Sir Edward Coke*.

[8] Coke was imprisoned for asserting parliament's right to debate all matters of concern to the commonwealth in the debate over freedom of speech, foreign policy, and Charles I's marriage in the 1621 parliament. Plans to send him to Ireland to prevent him sitting in 1624 failed; but in 1626 he was pricked as a sheriff, which prevented him from sitting in parliament.

[9] J. G. A. Pocock, *The Ancient Constitution and the Feudal Law: a Study of English Historical Thought in the Seventeenth Century. A Reissue with a Retrospect* (Cambridge, 1987); A. Cromartie, *The Constitutionalist Revolution: an Essay on the History of England, 1450–1642* (Cambridge, 2006).

[10] A. Cromartie, 'The constitutionalist revolution: the transformation of political culture in early Stuart England', *Past & Present*, clxiii (1999), 76–120, at pp. 87–8, 100; G. Burgess, *Absolute Monarchy and the Stuart Constitution* (New Haven, Conn., 1996), pp. 166–71.

1620s. Coke became more and more concerned to assert the law's control over, or at least bounding of, royal prerogative,[11] and Magna Carta was one exhibit in that argument: he famously declared that 'Magna Carta is such a fellow that he will have no sovereign'.[12] His parliamentary activities culminated in his role in the creation of the Petition of Right in 1628. The Petition invoked the Magna Carta of 1225 and other ancient statutes, including those confirming it, to assert the need for due legal process and protest against the recent use of imprisonment without cause shown.[13] The Petition of Right may have taken aim at specific grievances of the war years of the 1620s, but by placing them within the framework of the common law, and asserting that these rights were pre-existent independently of the grace of the monarch, it became a broader assertion of the rule of the law and the ancient constitution. The Petition of Right itself thus duly took its place in the pantheon of constitutional protections alongside Magna Carta for many civil war parliamentarians.

Scholars such as Christianson have rightly warned against seeing Coke as typical, and against seeing the common law as a field whose practitioners held uniform and uncritical views.[14] But if not typical, Coke was nonetheless influential, not least on the Leveller authors of the civil war period. Coke's distinctive shaping of the common law tradition, and his interpretation of Magna Carta's place in it, meant that Magna Carta and the materials of the common law were still surprisingly fertile for civil war radicals. For Coke, the common law was remarkably malleable. It was interpreted by the artificial 'reason' of common lawyers – a professional expertise which Coke was keen to guard, but which more radical followers would later blur into a more generalized 'reason'. Coke's own interpretations of legal texts sometimes had a noticeable political spin, often achieved by expanding the application of terms within the texts. He might even coin new 'maxims' rather than relying on those traditionally used to interpret the law.[15] The *Institutes of the Laws of England*, written in the turbulent 1620s, bequeathed these tendentious interpretations for use by the civil war parliamentarians,

---

[11] Burgess, *Absolute Monarchy*, pp. 200–1; White, *Sir Edward Coke*, pp. 219ff; Cromartie, *The Constitutionalist Revolution*, pp. 213–6.

[12] A. D. Boyer, 'Coke, Sir Edward (1552–1634)', *Oxford Dictionary of National Biography* (Oxford, 2004); online edn, Jan 2009 <https://doi.org/10.1093/ref:odnb/5826> [accessed 12 Dec. 2016].

[13] White, *Sir Edward Coke*, pp. 238–42.

[14] P. Christianson, 'Ancient constitutions', pp. 108–15, 145.

[15] C. Hill, *Intellectual Origins of the English Revolution Revisited* (Oxford, 1997), pp. 224–5; White, *Sir Edward Coke*, p. 226; Pocock, *The Ancient Constitution*, p. 268; A. Cromartie, *Sir Matthew Hale* (Cambridge, 1995), p. 19; J. W. Tubbs, *The Common Law Mind* (Baltimore , Md. and London, 2000), pp. 174–5.

in spite of the seizure of Coke's papers on Charles I's orders before Coke's death in 1634. It was the rebellious parliament which ensured that the remaining parts of Coke's *Institutes* were finally recovered and published. The second part of the *Institutes*, in which Coke's text and commentary on Magna Carta took pride of place at the very beginning of the book, was issued by the authority of parliament in 1642. Magna Carta, and Coke's interpretation of it, was thus published in support of the parliamentarian cause.

On one level, it is hard to see what Magna Carta had to offer to the parliamentarian thinkers of the English Civil War. Magna Carta is a compendious and various document, and many of its provisions, from fish weirs to wine measures, were very particular and specific to their time. Perhaps its most striking provision is the startling 'security clause' (clause 61 in the standard numbering) which constituted a corporate body of twenty-five named barons 'with the commune of all the land' to police the keeping of Magna Carta through force. Out of the whole of Magna Carta, the security clause ought to have been the most relevant to the English Civil War parliamentarians and even the radical Levellers. The key themes of parliamentarian political thought were precisely these issues: the procedures by which the king could be resisted, and the authority which was necessary for any bodies to undertake this political resistance. The Levellers had taken parliamentarian thought a step further, arguing not only that parliament could resist the king, but also that the people could resist a misbehaving parliament. And yet the security clause, like the vast majority of the provisions of Magna Carta, was not a feature of civil war propaganda, and makes no appearance at all in the Levellers' writings, for one very simple reason. Magna Carta, as published in Coke's *Institutes*, was not the Magna Carta of 1215; it was Henry III's reissued Great Charter of 1225, which had become the standard version of the text by the end of the thirteenth century. So, although Magna Carta came with associations of resistance and holding a king to account, Coke's widely cited text from 1225 did not lay out a system for limiting the king and policing his actions as the 1215 version had done.

Nevertheless, Coke still credited Magna Carta with immense power. He explained its title as the 'Great Charter' with a suitably hyperbolical comparison to Alexander the Great, who, he said, was called great 'not in respect of the largenesse of his body, for he was a little man, but in respect of the greatnesse of his heroicall spirit'.[16] Coke inflated Magna Carta's 'heroicall

---

[16] Edward Coke, *The Second Part of the Institutes of the Lawes of England* (1642) (hereafter 'Coke, *Second Institutes*'), 'A Proeme', unpaginated.

spirit' in an interpretation which laboured to derive broad principles from the Charter's apparently quite specific and historically contingent provisions. The most resonant chapter of Magna Carta, in the seventeenth century as now, was chapter 29 – in the 1225 version – which dealt with fair judicial procedures against individuals. This famously promised that no free man would be disseized of his 'liberties'. Coke elaborated enthusiastically on the several 'significations' of the term 'liberties', broadening the meaning of term far beyond particular legal entitlements. In one of those 'significations', 'liberties' simply meant 'the laws of the realme'.[17] Thus the liberties of the free man were expanded to include both specific liberties never thought of by the framers of Magna Carta (such as freedom from monopolies[18]), and the laws of the land themselves. This is why Coke could argue that Magna Carta 'made people free' ('liberos facit') and could be described as the charter of the liberties of the realm or even just as 'common freedom' ('communis libertas').[19] What was more, Magna Carta lay firmly within the resilient but flexible fabric of the customary common law of England: 'for the most part' it was 'declaratory of the principall grounds of the Fundamental Laws of England', and it was 'no new declaration' in 1225 as King John had previously declared the like. Magna Carta reached back beyond 1225 and even (implicitly) beyond 1215, and when kings, like Edward I, later confirmed it they were not making new law but just confirming that it 'should be taken as the Common Law'. Kings who thought better of having granted Magna Carta and attempted to cancel it were thus committing a category error: no king could cancel 'the ancient Common Law of England'. For Coke, that common law extended back before the Norman Conquest, and kings since the Conquest were still 'bound and sworn' to obey it.[20] Coke's interpretation of Magna Carta had woven new potential into the living fabric of the common law.

The Levellers, Coke and Magna Carta

Parliament fought a civil war against Charles I, and by 1646 it had won. It was in this year that the Leveller leaders began to work together as a group to push for a political settlement which fulfilled radical aims, both in religion and in politics. The Levellers were committed and enthusiastic

---

[17] Coke, *Second Institutes*, p. 47; P. Wende, '"Liberty" und "property" in der politischen Theorie der Levellers: ein Beitrag zur Entstehungsgeschichte der politischen Individualismus im England des 17. Jahrhunderts', *Zeitschrift für historische Forschung*, i (1974), 147–73, at p. 159.

[18] Coke, *Second Institutes*, p. 47.

[19] Coke, *Second Institutes*, 'Proeme'.

[20] Coke, *Second Institutes*, 'Proeme'.

parliamentarians, but they were at the radical end of a spectrum of views within the parliamentarian coalition. This coalition had already been fracturing during the fighting of the war, but in victory – with the task of trying to conclude a settlement with the defeated king – the divisions became even more evident. There were major differences among parliamentarians about whether to enforce membership of a reshaped national church, and about how extensive restrictions on the restored king's power should be. In the end, the army blocked a moderate settlement by purging parliament, leaving the more radical M.P.s to vote for the trial of the king. Charles I was tried and executed in January 1649.

The Levellers had certainly played a part in the radicalization of parliamentarian thought, denouncing regal tyranny and opening up the possibility of parliamentary rule without a king. They had taken parliament's justifications for leading resistance against the king – the idea that parliament represented the people and that politics was based on the consent of the ruled – and extended them. They wanted a much wider section of the adult male population to be actively represented in parliament, and they wanted parliament to be accountable to its electors. Thus as well as opposing the tyranny of kings, the Levellers opposed the potential tyranny of parliament itself. They had, like much of the population, been increasingly disillusioned by the behaviour of the Long Parliament, which had had to use methods as unpopular as those of the king in order to fund its war effort and run the country in the aftermath of war. The Leveller leaders, in addition, had particular reason to fear parliamentary 'tyranny' as two of them, John Lilburne and Richard Overton, experienced imprisonment on political grounds under parliamentary rule, even before the watershed of the regicide left the Levellers as major critics of the 'new chains' imposed on the nation by the new republican regime.

At first glance, it would seem that the Levellers' attitude to law, history and Magna Carta would be completely different from Sir Edward Coke's. The key leaders and pamphleteers of the Leveller movement were collaborating from 1645, and from 1647–9 the movement was at its peak. The fundamental basis of the Levellers' thought was the political equality of (adult, male) Englishmen, and the fact that there were certain rights and liberties which these citizens could not be stripped of and could always exercise. All political power, ultimately, had to derive from these 'free-born Englishmen', and all political authorities had to recognize that and be accountable to the people. For that reason, the Levellers' ideal constitution would look rather different from the institutions in place before the civil war: there would be a single-chamber elected 'Representative' instead of the two-chamber parliament of lords and commons; there might not even be a

The names of the Iury.
of life and death.

Figure 6.1. John Lilburne reading from Coke's Institutes at his
trial for treason (British Library shelfmark C.37.d.51.(5.)).

king or a house of lords. Certainly neither king nor lords would have a veto
on legislation; any king would have to be a mere executive officer. In their
tract *Regal Tyranny Discovered* in January 1647 the (anonymous) Leveller
authors railed not just against the monarchy of Charles I but against
monarchy itself, and particularly all the kings since the Norman Conquest.

On what grounds did the Levellers argue for such radical changes?
Natural law theory offered one kind of justification. This emphasized
people's original liberty and equality in the 'state of nature' and the contracts
which they had made. On this view, at some point in the distant past the
people had handed over some of their rights, at least conditionally, in return
for the security provided by government. The Levellers certainly made use

of this type of theory, although they emphasized that aspects of people's original liberty and equality persisted even in modern society, and that consent to government had not just happened in the distant past, but was also expressed through elections to the parliament or representative. The Levellers' proposals for far-reaching constitutional reform, and the theory of natural law which they sometimes used to justify them, seem strikingly modern – a long way from Coke's nostalgic appreciation of Magna Carta as part of an unbroken 'ancient constitution'. We might expect the Levellers to see arguments for the ancient constitution, and a reliance on Magna Carta, as rather inadequate to the serious task of reform which they thought was necessary.

Moreover, William Walwyn, one of the three most important Leveller leaders and thinkers, expressed exactly the kind of views of Magna Carta which we might expect. Just at the moment when the Leveller leaders were beginning to encounter each other and work together, Walwyn argued with his new acquaintance John Lilburne over the significance of the charter. Lilburne, imprisoned, and making the most of his martyrdom as he always did, was in 1645 wholeheartedly appealing to Magna Carta, apparently declaring grandly in a speech to the Committee of Examinations: 'Sir, the Privileges contained herein is my Birth-right and Inheritance'.[21] Walwyn, a man of wider intellectual horizons than Lilburne, found Lilburne's perspective problematic, and issued a famous rebuke to him, in a work of October 1645 called *Englands Lamentable Slaverie*. This was written as a letter to Lilburne and published in support of Lilburne's case. In it, Walwyn said that Magna Carta was 'but a part of the peoples rights and liberties' and was so narrow in its provisions for freedom that it was only 'deceitfully and improperlie Called Magna Charta, (indeed so called to blind the people)'. For Walwyn, Magna Carta was a small set of concessions 'wrestled out of the pawes of' (Norman) conquerors; indeed it was 'so little as lesse could not be granted with any pretence of freedom'. So much for it being the 'Great' Charter. For Walwyn at this time, Magna Carta was merely a concession on the part of kings. Not only had it been granted by kings, but both they and parliaments had subsequently done much to abbreviate the liberties contained in it: Walwyn clearly did not feel that Magna Carta in the present had much legal protection to offer. Even so, when danger appeared, these hypocritical parliaments could look no further than Magna Carta, 'calling that messe of pottage their birthright, the great inheritance of the people, the great Charter of England'. And of course, Walwyn was not just accusing parliaments of treating Magna Carta with too much reverence: he then

[21] John Lilburne, *The Copy of a Letter … to a Freind* (1645).

addressed Lilburne directly, saying 'Magna Charta hath been more precious in your esteeme then it deserveth'. He even urged that instead of fetishizing Magna Carta, parliament should legislate afresh: he complained that parliament, 'when they might have made a newer and better Charter, have falne to patching the old'.[22] This startling proposal for a completely new Magna Carta seems like another proof of Walwyn's willingness to abandon history for measures based purely on reason and current necessities. It was probably Walwyn who continued to criticize Magna Carta the following year, castigating it as 'but a beggerly thing, containing many marks of intollerable bondage' and arguing that the only guide for any government should be 'equity and right reason'.[23]

Lilburne initially seemed sensitive to Walwyn's critique, offering a commentary on how he viewed Magna Carta and English history in his pamphlet *The Iust Mans Justification* the next summer. But even there, he did not completely concede Walwyn's points – although he went some way towards it – and he continued to appeal to Magna Carta. In 1647 he even issued a substantial pamphlet which summarized Magna Carta and other key statutes 'for the instruction, information and benefit of all true-hearted Englishmen'.[24] He clearly still thought it had something to offer. Out of the three Leveller leaders, Lilburne was the most inclined to make use of legal language and arguments. However, the third major Leveller writer, Richard Overton, who was responsible for some of the Levellers' most resounding statements of natural law theory, also rhapsodized about Magna Carta. Indeed, on one occasion in November 1646 he claims to have defended his copy of it physically, while being recommitted to prison in Newgate after an unsuccessful hearing before a committee of the house of commons. When his gaoler attempted to seize the book – which was of course the second volume of Coke's *Institutes* – Overton

> replyed, that he should not, if to the utmost of my power I could preserve it from him, and I would do my utmost, where upon I clapped it in my Armes, and I laid myself on my belly, but by force, they violently turned me upon my back then Briscoe (just as if he had been staving off a Dog from the Beare) smote me with his fist, to make me let go my hold, whereupon as loud as I

---

[22] William Walwyn, *Englands Lamentable Slaverie* (1645), in *The Writings of William Walwyn*, ed. J. R. McMichael and B. Taft (Athens, Ga., 1989), pp. 147–8.

[23] *A Remonstrance of Many Thousand Citizens* (1646), p. 15. This seminal Leveller pamphlet often used to be attributed to Richard Overton by scholars, but David Adams has demonstrated that Overton printed but probably did not write it. Walwyn thus seems the most likely candidate for authorship (D. R. Adams, 'The secret printing and publishing career of Richard Overton the Leveller, 1644–46', *The Library*, xi (2010), 3–88).

[24] John Lilburne, *The Peoples Prerogative* (1648), title page.

could, I cryed out, murther, murther, murther. And thus by an assault they got the great Charter of *Englands Liberties and Freedoms* from me; which I laboured to the utmost power in me, to preserve and defend, and ever to the death shall maintain, and forthwith without any Warrant poore Magna Charta was clapt up close prisoner in Newgate, and my poore fellow prisoner de[p]rived of the comfortable visitation of friends: And thus [I was] stript of my armour of proofe, the Charter of my legall Rights, Freedomes and Liberties ...'[25]

That story of Overton's gives us one of the reasons why the Levellers continued to appeal to Magna Carta: it was useful as a proof-text for the legally self-taught but rhetorically skilful Leveller leaders when they found themselves – as Lilburne especially often did – in prison. The fact that their prolonged imprisonments were initially on the order of the house of lords, and did not lead to trials at common law, meant that the provisions of Magna Carta could be a real help to their case. The Levellers were interested in very few of the specific provisions of the Great Charter. They focused overwhelmingly on chapter 29 of the 1225 charter (a chapter to which Coke had devoted a full twelve pages of his seventy-eight-page commentary). This chapter combined the famous provisions of chapters 39–40 of the original 1215 charter, and thus gave protection to every 'liber homo', free person or free man, against punishment in person or property inflicted by the state 'except by the lawful judgement of his peers or the law of the land'. These provisions – especially combined with Coke's glosses on them – were directly useful to the imprisoned Levellers. Overton, for example, transcribed Coke's commentary exactly when he insisted that any judgement leading to imprisonment must be made by a man's peers or equals – 'that is men of his own condition'. Similarly, 'the law of the land' was glossed so that it referred not just to the laws which subjects might be judged for transgressing, but to the whole legal mechanism of due process. Coke made this point emphatically, and again Overton transcribed it exactly: 'by the law of the land (that is, to speak it once for all) by the due course, and processe of law'.[26] For Lilburne – following Coke – Magna Carta guaranteed law, justice and right – 'the best Birth-right the Subject hath'.[27] Lilburne also frequently specifically cited chapter 29 of the 1225 charter, and material from Coke both on the significance of that chapter and on the importance and meaning of judgement by one's peers.[28] Even in his pamphlet *The Peoples Prerogative*, which proclaimed prominently on

[25] Richard Overton, *The Commoners Complaint* (1647), p. 14.
[26] Richard Overton, *An Arrow Against All Tyrants and Tyranny* (1646), pp. 6–7; Coke, *Second Institutes*, p. 46.
[27] John Lilburne, *Innocency and Truth Justified* (1646), p. 64; Coke, *Second Institutes*, p. 56.
[28] For example, John Lilburne, *The Oppressed Mans Oppressions* (1647), p. 24.

its title page that it was 'a collection of the Marrow and Soule of Magna Charta' (Magna Carta was evidently a big 'seller' in the 1640s as now), he actually began the pamphlet not with Magna Carta itself but with the Petition of Right; and when he moved on to Magna Carta he introduced only four chapters: 14, 26, 28 and 29, which dealt again with Lilburne's characteristic concerns of judgement by one's peers, the need for witnesses, and due process of law. In fact, in a pamphlet which had 'Magna Carta' emblazoned very prominently on its title page, he spent less than a page on Magna Carta before moving on to the liberties guaranteed by more recent statutes.[29]

But beyond this practical use of Magna Carta, there were deeper reasons why the Levellers, even after Walwyn's compelling and fundamentally historically accurate critique of the imposition of Norman law and custom, still returned to the language of law and to Magna Carta, that concession offered by Norman kings. Magna Carta, particularly as interpreted by Coke, came to represent 'the liberties of England', and in spite of the Levellers' vitriol against the Norman kings, the implication that these liberties were still guaranteed by a continuing web of law and English rights was enormously useful. As Martin Dzelzainis has pointed out, the Levellers' appeals to common law have to be seen in the light of the Long Parliament's reputation and thought in the 1640s. As parliament lost its claim to be the defender of the law, and some of its propagandists moved towards accepting a kind of parliamentary absolutism, the Levellers moved in the opposite direction, invoking Magna Carta as a defence of the people's rights against their parliament as well as against their king.[30] And while we tend to separate out the 'languages of political thought' used in civil war argument, at the time they were cheerfully combined by many authors, and particularly by Lilburne. Lilburne did use the language of the law, but he used it very creatively. He talked about 'liberties', 'franchises', 'privileges' and 'immunities' – specific entitlements which people enjoyed because of specific grants made to them or because of the particular status or office which they held. But Lilburne used these terms in a way which changed their inherited legal meaning in a fundamental way. For him, all 'free-born Englishmen' enjoyed the same collection of liberties and rights, simply through being born in England. (The non-free status of villeinage was no longer in existence, and when Lilburne and others talked of 'free-born Englishmen' it was to emphasize the fact that *all* Englishmen were

[29] Lilburne, *The Peoples Prerogative*, pp. 4–6.
[30] M. Dzelzainis, 'History and ideology: Milton, the Levellers, and the Council of State in 1649', *Huntington Library Quarterly*, lxviii (2005), pp. 269–87.

free.[31]) The Leveller belief in extensive political equality, which transcended many (though not all) kinds of social inequality, thus resulted in a vision of equal liberties and rights which Englishmen enjoyed. Lilburne had used the materials of the law to create a kind of citizenship. Thus Lilburne used the language of the law to construct an account of the (legal) liberties of the 'free-born Englishman' which converged with the Leveller writers' account of the liberties accorded to all men by natural law. Lilburne was capable of appealing to 'national and natural, rational and legal' laws in one breath. The radicalism of the Levellers clearly did not lie in a rejection of history and law. Rather, it lay in a fascinating synthesis of legal and historical thought with the abstract principles of natural law.[32]

I want to conclude with a final speculation about the place of Magna Carta in the Levellers' thought. The Levellers embodied many of their demands in petitions, but also adopted the idea of an 'Agreement of the People', a document outlining the powers of the parliament and the people which would be subscribed by the people of England to legitimize it as a settlement. This idea did not originate directly from the Leveller movement, and was not confined to it either: a series of proposals for an 'Agreement of the People' was produced by army radicals, Levellers and army officers. Those conventionally called the first and third Agreements of the People (October/November 1647 and May 1649) were the work of radicals; the second Agreement (December/January 1648–9) was the contested product of negotiations between radicals and the army leadership in the period between the army's purging of parliament and the trial of Charles I. The first 'Agreement of the People' in 1647 was produced for the Putney Debates by army radicals and displays a mixture of Leveller and army concerns.[33] It was an audaciously simple document, which proposed that the nation was to be ruled by a succession of frequently re-elected parliaments or 'Representatives', whose power was to be 'inferior only to theirs who chose them'. These parliaments were to hold many of the marks of sovereignty previously seen as belonging to the king's prerogative, but the people reserved certain powers to themselves. Thus the parliament could not make laws to bind people to particular forms of worship, or any law which was against the good of the people and no-one

---

[31] K. Thomas, 'The Levellers and the franchise', in *The Interregnum: the Quest for Settlement 1646–1660*, ed. G. E. Aylmer (1972), pp. 57–78, at pp. 73–5.

[32] For a more detailed discussion of the issues in this paragraph, see R. Foxley, 'John Lilburne and the citizenship of "free-born Englishmen"', *Hist. Jour.*, xlvii (2004), 849–74.

[33] E. Vernon and P. Baker, 'What was the first Agreement of the People?', *Hist. Jour.*, liii (2010), 39–60; *The Agreements of the People, the Levellers and the Constitutional Crisis of the English Revolution*, ed. P. Baker and E. Vernon (Basingstoke, 2012).

was to be exempt from the law because of any particular status or privilege they enjoyed.

The device of an Agreement subscribed by the people has seemed to place the Levellers and their radical allies in the army who produced the first Agreement firmly in the natural law tradition. Several historians have interpreted the Agreement of the People itself as a new 'social contract';[34] perhaps this was what Walwyn had meant when he argued in favour of making a 'new Charter' instead of continuing to patch up the inadequate Magna Carta. However, the first two Agreements of the People do not actually cut themselves off from history in quite such a simple way. As Alan Orr has argued, the *Agreements* can be read as vindications of existing right, in the tradition of medieval constitutionalism, rather than as documents creating new rights.[35] The short conclusion to the first Agreement's text clarified the position of the Agreement in English constitutional history: the authors were determined to vindicate their rights, inspired by the example of 'our Ancestors, whose bloud was often spent in vain for the recovery of their Freedomes, suffering themselves, through fradulent [*sic*] accommodations, to be still deluded of the fruit of their Victories'. The same was not to happen this time round. The ancient cycle of assertion and suppression of these 'native Rights' was finally to come to an end with a definitive, unalterable codification.[36] The Agreement was thus conceived of as momentous, but it placed itself within the nation's history rather than cutting itself off from it. Like Magna Carta, the Agreement, once agreed by the population, could not be changed by parliament; it would be a fundamental law. That fundamental law, however, was designed to confirm and protect the existing 'native rights' of the English people. Some of those fundamental rights were still to be found in Magna Carta too. I suggest that the Agreement of the People was thus a tribute and a successor to Magna Carta, rather than simply a replacement.

---

[34] J. Frank, *The Levellers: a History of the Writings of Three Seventeenth-Century Social Democrats: John Lilburne, Richard Overton, William Walwyn* (Cambridge, Mass., 1955), p. 142; H. N. Brailsford, *The Levellers and the English Revolution* (1961), p. 376; I. Hampsher-Monk, 'The political theory of the Levellers: Putney, property and Professor Macpherson', *Political Studies*, xxiv (1976), 397–422, at p. 417. For a fuller discussion of the natural law aspects of Leveller thought and of the idea of the Agreements of the People as social contracts, see R. Foxley, *The Levellers: Radical Political Thought in the English Revolution* (Manchester, 2013), chs. 1 and 2.

[35] D. A. Orr, 'Constitutionalism: ancient, modern and early modern in the *Agreements of the People*', in Baker and Vernon, *The Agreements of the People*, pp. 76–96.

[36] *An Agreement of the People for a Firme and Present Peace* (1647), pp. 5–6.

7. Magna Carta in the American Revolution

Harry T. Dickinson

In the 1760s the political disputes between Britain and its American colonies developed into a revolutionary crisis, which eventually led to war and the creation of an independent United States of America. In this crisis, which was primarily political and constitutional, the colonists challenged the authority of the British government and the power of the Westminster parliament by appealing to the notion of fundamental law, the principles of the English common law, the liberties granted to them in their colonial charters, and their understanding of England's ancient constitution. In doing so, they frequently appealed to the rights and liberties granted by Magna Carta according to the interpretation of this charter of liberties that had been advanced over the centuries and more recently by Edward Coke and his allies who had strenuously defended the liberties of the subject and the rule of law against Stuart absolutism in the early seventeenth century. In the early thirteenth century Magna Carta had been supported by a baronial elite anxious to preserve its feudal privileges. It had not protected the rights and liberties of all the king's subjects and it had not effectively limited the powers of the crown.[1] Over the next four centuries, however, frequent confirmations of it by kings and parliaments,[2] reinterpretations of it by teachers in the Inns of Court and by judges and lawyers appealing to it in numerous trials,[3] and political exploitations of it by opponents of the crown's prerogatives had seen its meaning and significance greatly expanded.[4]

[1] E. Jenks, 'The myth of Magna Carta', *Independent Rev.*, iv (1905), 260–73; S. Painter, 'Magna Carta', *American Hist. Rev.*, liii (1947), 42–9; C. H. McIlwain, 'Due process of law in Magna Carta', *Columbia Law Rev.*, xiv (1914), 27–51; and W. S. McKechnie, *Magna Carta: a Commentary on the Great Charter of King John* (2nd edn., Glasgow, 1914).

[2] F. Thompson, *The First Century of Magna Carta: Why it Persisted as a Document* (Minneapolis, Minn., 1925); F. Thompson, 'Parliamentary confirmations of the Great Charter', *American Hist. Rev.*, xxxviii (1933), 659–72; and F. Thompson, *Magna Carta: its Role in the Making of the English Constitution 1300–1629* (Minneapolis, Minn., 1948).

[3] Thompson, *Magna Carta: its Role in the Making of the English Constitution*, pp. 167–96 and 268–93; and *Selected Readings and Commentaries on Magna Carta 1400–1604*, ed. J. Baker (Selden Soc., cxxxii, 2015).

[4] Thompson, *Magna Carta: its Role in the Making of the English Constitution*, pp. 335–53; C. H. McIlwain, 'Magna Carta and the common law', in *Magna Carta: Commemorative*

H.T. Dickinson, 'Magna Carta and the American Revolution', in *Magna Carta: history, context and influence*, ed. L. Goldman (2018), pp. 79–100.

By the later seventeenth century there was widespread support for Magna Carta, in both England and in the American colonies, but appeals were now made to the Magna Carta which had been interpreted and expanded over the centuries and mediated in particular by Edward Coke and his allies in the early seventeenth century, not to the Magna Carta of 1215 or even to that of 1225.[5] It was now widely assumed that Magna Carta had guaranteed that justice would not be sold, delayed or denied to any subject, and that all accused persons must know the charge levelled against them, must be speedily brought to face their accusers and be free to offer their defence in an open trial conducted according to the law of the land and before a jury of their equals in the vicinity of where the offence had taken place. It was further widely believed that Magna Carta was a fundamental law designed to preserve England's ancient constitution and immemorial common law by bringing all powers, even the royal prerogative, under the rule of law and denying parliament the right to pass statutes contrary to fundamental laws of this kind.

Throughout the American crisis of the later eighteenth century the colonists repeatedly insisted that their charters from the king had always granted them the same rights and liberties as their fellow subjects back home in England, including those granted by Magna Carta. They pointed to the Virginia charter of 1606, which had promised that the emigrants who settled in this colony, and their descendants, 'shall have and enjoy all Liberties, Franchises, and Immunities as if they had been abiding and born, within this our realm of England'.[6] Similar rights were granted to many other colonies in America, from Massachusetts in 1629 to Georgia in 1732.[7] The colonists themselves were generally very willing to adopt the English common law and English legal practices. When dissatisfied with

---

Essays, ed. H. E. Malden (1917), pp. 122–79; J. R. Maddicott, 'Magna Carta and the local community', *Past & Present*, cii (1984), 25–65; D. Carpenter, 'English peasants in politics, 1258–1267', *Past & Present*, cxxxvi (1992), 3–42; S. T. Ambler, 'Magna Carta: its confirmation at Simon de Montfort's parliament of 1265', *Eng. Hist Rev.*, cxxx (2015), 801–30; M. Ashley, *Magna Carta in the Seventeenth Century* (Charlottesville, Va., 1965); and J. G. A. Pocock, *The Ancient Constitution and the Feudal Law: a Study of English Historical Thought in the Seventeenth Century* (2nd edn., Cambridge, 1987).

[5] King John had agreed to accept Magna Carta at a meeting with his rebellious barons at Runnymede in June 1215, but within ten weeks he had revoked it and Pope Innocent III had annulled it. This decision had led to civil war. In 1225 John's son, Henry III, had voluntarily reissued a revised and shortened version of Magna Carta. This version was the one frequently reissued and confirmed thereafter.

[6] *The Federal and State Constitutions*, ed. F. N. Thorpe (7 vols., Washington D.C., 1909), vii. 3788; and A. E. Dick Howard, *The Road from Runnymede: Magna Carta and Constitutionalism in America* (Charlottesville, Va., 1968), pp. 15, 19.

[7] Dick Howard, *The Road from Runnymede*, p. 25.

the government of their colony, they frequently attempted to redress their grievances by appealing to the rights of Englishmen, including those they believed were enshrined in Magna Carta. The Maryland legislative assembly passed a law in 1638 which granted that the 'Inhabitants of this province shall have all their rights and liberties according to the great charter of England' and appeals were made to Magna Carta in a number of lawsuits contested in the Maryland courts.[8] In Massachusetts a 'Body of Liberties' was drawn up in 1641 stressing the right of all the colony's inhabitants to trial by jury, due legal process, and equal justice. All these liberties were drawn directly from chapter 29 of the 1225 version of Magna Carta. In 1646 the general court of Massachusetts claimed that the laws of the colony were in accord with Magna Carta. Two years later, the 'Laws and Liberties of Massachusetts' laid down several legal provisions, which were again drawn directly from chapter 29 of Magna Carta.[9] William Penn, the first proprietor of the colony of Pennsylvania, successfully appealed to Magna Carta, when he demanded to know what specific law he had broken, when he was charged in London with disturbing the peace. He did not abandon his principles when he settled in America. In 1681, he drafted a charter for Pennsylvania and Delaware that guaranteed the inhabitants of these colonies a fair trial and freedom from unjust imprisonment. In 1687 he arranged for the first printing in America of the 1225 version of Magna Carta and also the 1297 confirmation of it, in his tract, *The Excellent Privilege of Liberty and Property: Being the Birth-Right of the Free-Born Subjects of England*.[10] Throughout the later eighteenth century, in their constitutional disputes with Britain, the American colonies continually reiterated that they possessed the same rights and liberties as the British people because of the grants made to them in their royal charters. In 1765, for example, Governor Stephen Hopkins of Rhode Island declared, 'By all these charters, it is in the most express and solemn manner granted that these adventurers [the English colonists in America], and their children after them forever, should have and enjoy all the freedom and liberty that the subjects in England enjoy'.[11] In 1766, Richard Bland appealed to Magna Carta as an earlier form of contract between the monarch and his subjects. He claimed that the rights and liberties enshrined in Magna Carta had been possessed by the English people since Anglo-Saxon times, long before 1215,

---

[8] Dick Howard, *The Road from Runnymede*, p. 54; and H. D. Hazeltine, 'The influence of Magna Carta on American constitutional development', *Columbia Law Rev.*, xvii (1917), 1–33, at p. 12.

[9] Dick Howard, *The Road from Runnymede*, pp. 37–48.

[10] Dick Howard, *The Road from Runnymede*, pp. 213–14; and *Magna Carta and the Rule of Law*, ed. D. B. Magraw, A. Martinez and R. Brownell II (Chicago, Ill. 2014), p. 160.

[11] Stephen Hopkins, *The Rights of the Colonies Examined* (Providence, R.I., 1765), p. 5.

and had been passed on to the American colonists as a fundamental law through their royal charters.[12] Thomas Jefferson also made the same point.[13] John Tucker maintained that the compact, created by royal charters, and reinforced by Magna Carta, limited the powers which George III could exercise over the American colonies. He claimed in 1771 that the American colonists lived under the British constitution, whose:

> constitutional laws are comprised in *Magna-Charta* [sic],[14] or the great charter of the nation. This contains, in general, the liberties and privileges of the people, and is, *virtually*, a compact between the king and them; the reigning Prince, explicitly engaging, by solemn oath, to govern according to the laws: – Beyond the extent of these then or contrary to them, he can have no rightful authority at all.[15]

Such colonial opinions were strongly contested in Britain, however. In seeking to impose its authority on the colonies the British government, supported by a clear majority in the Westminster parliament, insisted that the supreme sovereign authority in Britain and also in all British North America lay with the combined legislature of the king, the house of lords and the house of commons. This view of the British constitution had been steadily developing since the Glorious Revolution of 1688–9. Whereas the American colonists appealed to an early seventeenth-century view of the English constitution, which raised the law above both the British executive and legislature, many British politicians, since the Glorious Revolution, had become convinced that the combined legislature at Westminster possessed the right to pass, amend or revoke any law and could even alter or repeal the rights and liberties granted by Magna Carta.[16] William Blackstone, the celebrated and highly influential jurist, had claimed in 1765 that each state needed 'a supreme, irresistible, absolute, uncontrolled authority', and, in Britain, he asserted, this was the combined legislature of king, lords and commons.[17] Even Edmund Burke, a politician very anxious to conciliate the American colonies, could never surrender his conviction that the British

[12] Richard Bland, *An Enquiry into the Rights of the British Colonies* (Williamsburg, 1766), cited in H. T. Colbourn, *The Lamp of Experience: Whig History and the Intellectual Origins of the American Revolution* (Chapel Hill, N.C., 1965), p. 147.

[13] S. R. Hauer, 'Thomas Jefferson and the Anglo-Saxon Language', *Publications of the Modern Language Association*, xcviii (183), 879–98.

[14] In the 18th century the great charter of liberty was often written as *Magna Charta*.

[15] John Tucker, *A Sermon preached at Cambridge [Massachusetts], before his Excellency Thomas Hutchinson, Esq, Governor* (Boston, Mass., 1771), p. 17.

[16] H. T. Dickinson, 'The eighteenth century debate on the sovereignty of parliament', *Trans. Royal Hist. Soc.*, 5th ser., xxvi (1976), 189–210.

[17] Willia Blackstone, *Commentaries on the Laws of England* (4 vols., Oxford, 1765–9), i. 49.

legislature was the supreme authority in America as it was in Britain.[18] By the 1760s, the British defenders of parliamentary sovereignty had abandoned the long-standing belief that parliament's sphere of action was limited by the superior authority of the fundamental law.[19] Josiah Tucker, a leading British critic of the colonists' claims, maintained that their arguments were self-defeating. He acknowledged that Magna Carta was the great foundation of English liberties and the basis of the constitution. It denied the king the right to raise taxes by his own prerogative and it supported the constitutional right of parliament alone to give consent to tax-raising measures. Magna Carta therefore supported the superior authority of parliament over that of the subordinate colonial legislative assemblies and hence it could not be appealed to in order to challenge the constitutional powers of parliament:

> the principal End and Intention of Magna Charta, as far as Taxation is concerned, was to assert the Authority and Jurisdiction of the three Estates of the kingdom [king, lords and commons], in Opposition to the sole Prerogative of the King; so that if you [the colonists] will now plead the Spirit of Magna Charta, against the Jurisdiction of Parliament, you will plead Magna Charta against itself.[20]

British defenders of parliamentary sovereignty also pointed out that not all the American colonies had been granted a royal charter of liberties. The royal charters that had been granted had not conferred on the colonists all the rights and liberties of Englishmen (the right to vote in parliamentary elections, for example).[21] Moreover, in the past, colonial charters had on several occasions been reviewed, altered and even revoked and, since they had been granted by the crown alone, they would always be subordinate to the sovereign authority of the British legislature.[22] William Blackstone conceded that, 'if an uninhabited country is discovered, and planted by

---

[18] H. T. Dickinson, 'America', in *The Cambridge Companion to Edmund Burke*, ed. D. W. Dwan and C. Insole (Cambridge, 2012), pp. 156–67.

[19] J. W. Gough, *Fundamental Law in English Constitutional History* (Oxford, 1955), pp. 174–213.

[20] Josiah Tucker, *A Letter from a Merchant in London to his Nephew in North America* (1766), p. 5. The same sentiment in exactly the same words can be found in William Pulteney, *Thoughts on the present state of affairs with America, and the means of conciliation* (1778), p. 86. See also *The Rights of Parliament vindicated, on the occasion of the late Stamp-Act, in which is exposed the conduct of the American Colonists* (1766), pp. 6, 14.

[21] H. T. Dickinson, 'Britain's imperial sovereignty: the ideological case against the American colonists', in *Britain and the American Revolution*, ed. H. T. Dickinson (1998), pp. 73–80.

[22] D. J. Hulsebosch, 'The ancient constitution and the extending empire: Sir Edward Coke's British jurisprudence', *Law and History Rev*, xxi (2003), 439–82, at pp. 475–82.

English subjects, all the British laws then in being, which are the birthright of every subject, are immediately there in force. For as the law is the birthright of every subject, so wherever they go, they carry their laws with them'.[23] Unfortunately for the colonial cause, however, he promptly went on to assert that, in territories which had been conquered or ceded by treaty, as was the case with all of Britain's American colonies, the common law of England had no authority there and the colonists inhabiting these territories were subject to the sovereign authority of the British legislature.[24] The American colonies might be allowed to possess their own legislatures, which could pass local laws, but these subordinate legislatures could not pass laws contrary to those passed by the Westminster parliament. On the other hand, the imperial Westminster parliament could pass laws for, and raise taxes in, the American colonies.[25] Ironically, in view of how much the colonists relied in the 1760s on many of the arguments advanced against arbitrary and oppressive power by Edward Coke in the early seventeenth century, Coke had himself maintained that those English subjects who left the realm of England to live in the American colonies could not claim the same rights and liberties, under the common law or according to Magna Carta, as those who remained in England.[26] This was one argument of Coke's that the American colonists ignored.

In defending what they regarded as their constitutional rights and liberties, and in resisting the British efforts in the 1760s and 1770s to impose imperial authority over them, the American colonists often appealed to Magna Carta as proof of their claims. On a number of occasions they used visual images of Magna Carta as a symbol of their right to claim the civil liberties possessed by Englishmen. In January 1766, Paul Revere, an engraver and silversmith, produced a graphic print, *A View of the Year 1765*, in which he depicted a Stamp Act dragon, supported by two devils, trying to snatch Magna Carta from a man representing Boston.[27] In 1768, Revere produced a beautiful silver punch bowl in honour of several leading 'Sons of Liberty' in Massachusetts. He decorated this with references to John Wilkes and his notorious publication, the *North Briton*, number 45, and added flags representing Magna Carta and the English Bill of Rights of 1689 on either side of this image. In the same year, the title page to the third edition of John Dickinson's influential political tract, *Letters from a*

[23] Blackstone, *Commentaries on the Laws of England*, i. 104–105.
[24] Blackstone, *Commentaries on the Laws of England*, i. 105.
[25] Dickinson, 'Britain's imperial sovereignty', pp. 86–94.
[26] Hulsebosch, 'The ancient constitution and the extending empire', pp. 439–40.
[27] See E. P. Richardson, 'Stamp act cartoons in the colonies', *Pennsylvania Magazine of History and Biography*, xcvi (1972), 275–97.

Figure 7.1. Seal of Massachusetts Bay Colony, 1775.
Courtesy of Massachusetts Archives, Boston.

Farmer in Pennsylvania, shows him standing with Magna Carta under his right elbow and a book by Sir Edward Coke on his bookshelf. In 1774, Paul Revere was commissioned by the *Royal American Magazine* to engrave the head and shoulders of both Sam Adams and John Hancock above a scroll labelled 'Magna Charta'. When the American patriots decided to publish the *Journal of the Proceedings of the [Continental] Congress held at Philadelphia, on 5 September 1774* the title-page was decorated with an image of twelve hands grasping in unison a pillar resting upon a base entitled Magna Carta. On 15 December 1774, the *New York Journal* was illustrated with a similar design, but this time intertwined snakes encircled it as further proof that the American patriots were establishing their political unity. In July 1775, Maryland published a four-dollar paper banknote, whose design included 'Liberty' handing a petition to 'Britannia', who is being restrained by King George III, who is shown trampling upon Magna Carta. Finally, the Great Seal of Massachusetts, designed in 1775, depicts a colonist holding a sword in his right hand and Magna Carta in his left hand.[28]

Interesting and important as such symbols were, they were not as significant or as influential in rallying the American colonists against British policies as the arguments produced in law courts, speeches, debates and printed publications. Many of these cited Magna Carta in support of colonial claims to their rights and liberties and their protests against Britain's misuse

[28] S. Hamilton, '"The earliest Device of the Colonies" and some other early devices', *Princeton University Library Chronicle*, x (1949), 117–23.

THE PATRIOTIC AMERICAN FARMER.
J-N D-K-NS——N Esq! BARRISTER at LAW:
Who with Attic Eloquence and Roman Spirit hath Asserted.
The Liberties of the BRITISH Colonies in America.

'Tis nobly done, to Stem Taxations 'Rage,
And raise, the thoughts of a degen'rate Age,
For Happiness, and Joy, from Freedom Spring,
But Life in Bondage, is a worthless Thing.

Printed for & Sold by R. Bell Bookseller

. Frontispiece, third edition, John Dickinson's *Letters from a Farmer in Penn-
!vania* (1768). Magna Carta appears under the right elbow, and *Coke upon
ttleton* on the shelf. (Courtesy, John Carter Brown Library, Brown Univer-
y.)

Figure 7.2. Frontispiece, "The Patriotic American Farmer"; i.e.,
3rd edn. of John Dickinson's *Letters from a Farmer in Pennsylvania*.
Courtesy of John Carter Brown Library, Brown University.

of its judicial, executive and legislative powers. As early as 1761, James Otis
challenged the right of the king's officials in Massachusetts to use 'writs
of assistance', a form of general warrant, allowing the examination of the
premises of Boston merchants on the mere suspicion that smuggled goods
might be located there. In winning his case, Otis appealed to Magna Carta
to support the argument that a specific charge needed to be made before
such an examination of private property could be undertaken.[29] When the

[29] Dick Howard, *The Road from Runnymede*, p. 133.

JOURNAL

OF THE

PROCEEDINGS

OF THE

CONGRESS,

Held at PHILADELPHIA,

September 5, 1774.

PHILADELPHIA:

Printed by WILLIAM and THOMAS BRADFORD,

at the *London Coffee-House.*

DCC,LXXIV.

Figure 7.3. Journal of the Proceedings of the Congress held at Philadelphia, 1774. Title page of book in British Library. © British Library Board, shelf mark C.38.f.33.

British parliament passed the Sugar Act in 1764, it determined that those colonists, who attempted to avoid paying customs or excise duties, would be prosecuted in a vice-admiralty court established at Halifax, Nova Scotia. There, the charges would not be heard by juries made up of local colonists, but by judges appointed by the crown. The Townshend Acts of 1767 established additional vice-admiralty courts in Boston, Philadelphia and Charleston, which were used even more frequently by customs collectors. The result was repeated protests that the colonists were being denied legal rights that were not being denied to Britons charged with smuggling offences.[30] A town meeting in Braintree, Massachusetts, in 1765, protested against the British attempt to use vice-admiralty courts to punish those who refused to pay taxes levied by the Westminster parliament, because such trials would not be heard by a jury, which was a policy 'directly repugnant to the Great Charter itself'.[31] In September 1765, the colonial legislature in Pennsylvania resolved: 'That the vesting an authority in the courts of admiralty to decide in suits relating to the stamp duties, and other matters, foreign to their jurisdiction, is highly dangerous to the liberties of his majesty's American subjects, contrary to Magna Charta, the great charter and fountain of English liberty, and destructive of one of their most *darling and acknowledged rights*, that of TRIALS BY JURIES'.[32] A month later, the lower house of the Connecticut legislature condemned the Sugar Act of 1764, on similar grounds. Vice-admiralty courts, used to prosecute those who tried to evade paying the sugar duty, were charged with being 'highly dangerous to the liberties of his Majesty's American subjects, contrary to the great charter of English liberty, and destructive of one of their most darling rights, that of trial by juries, which is justly esteemed one chief excellence of the British Constitution'.[33] In February 1766, the Sons of Liberty held a mock trial for the Stamp Act, in which the prisoner was found 'guilty of a Breach of the Magna Charta, and a design to subvert the British constitution'.[34]

In order to restrict the use of such prerogative courts, under the influence of the British executive, the legislative assemblies in several colonies began erecting their own courts and appointing their own judges so that judicial decisions in such cases could be resolved outside the king's vice-admiralty courts. These courts advanced petitions against the oppressive use of the king's courts and pressed for legislative action to be taken in the colonial assemblies without seeking the consent of the king.[35] In June 1768, when John Hancock was prosecuted in the vice-admiralty court in Boston for failing to get a permit to unload cargo from his sloop, *Liberty*, John Adams, the future second president of the United States, successfully defended him by

---

[30] D. S. Lovejoy, '"Rights imply equality": the case against admiralty jurisdiction in America, 1764–1776', *William and Mary Quarterly*, 3rd ser., xvi (1959), 459–84.

[31] J. L. Malcolm, 'Magna Carta in America: entrenched', in *Magna Carta: the Foundation of Freedom 1215–2015*, ed. N. Vincent (2nd edn., 2015), p. 125.

[32] *The Proceedings of the North American Colonies in consequence of the Stamp Act* (1766), p. 10; and *Prologue to Revolution: Sources and Documents on the Stamp Act Crisis, 1764–1766*, ed. E. S. Morgan (Chapel Hill, N.C., 1959), p. 52.

[33] *The Public Records of the Colony of Connecticut*, ed. C. J. Headley and J. H. Trumbull (15 vols., Hartford, Conn, 1881–90), xii. 424; and Morgan, *Prologue to Revolution*, p. 55.

[34] *Boston Gazette*, 24 February 1766.

[35] Magraw *et al.*, *Magna Carta and the Rule of Law*, pp. 66–8.

maintaining that this prosecution was against the legal principles enshrined in chapter 29 of the 1225 version of Magna Carta.[36] Adams highlighted and condemned the distinction that the Westminster parliament's legislation had made between British subjects and American colonists:

> What shall we say to this distinction? Is there not in this clause, a Brand of Infamy, of Degradation, and Disgrace, fixed upon every American? Is he not degraded below the Rank of an Englishman? Is it not directly a Repeal of Magna Charta, as far as America Is concerned ... This 29 Chap. of Magna Charta has for many Centuries been esteemed by Englishmen, as one of the noblest Monuments one of the firmest Bullwarks of their Liberties ... The [Sugar Act] takes from Mr Hancock this precious Tryal Per Legem Terra [by the law of the land], and gives it to a single Judge. However respectable the Judge may be, it is however an Hardship and severity, which distinguishes my Clyent from the rest of Englishmen.[37]

When, in 1772, Britain attempted to put on trial far outside the colony those colonists charged with burning one of his majesty's revenue ships, which was endeavouring to prevent smuggling in the colonies, Chief Justice Stephen Hopkins of Rhode Island successfully maintained that such an action would be a violation of the right enshrined in Magna Carta that any accused person should always be tried by a jury composed of men living in the vicinity of where the crime took place.[38] After the Boston Tea Party of 16 December 1773, when some colonists attacked British merchant ships importing tea into the colony, the British parliament passed the Intolerable or Coercive Acts of 1774 to punish Massachusetts. Of these, the Administration of Justice Act allowed the British authorities to prosecute anyone accused of attacking the property of British merchants in trials held far outside the American colonies. Leading American patriots, including Thomas Jefferson, protested that it was contrary to Magna Carta and the common law to hold a trial outside the locality where the offence took place.[39] When leading American colonists convened to discuss how to unite in opposition to Britain's imperial policies in the First Continental Congress held in Philadelphia, in October 1774, they passed resolutions insisting that the colonists had inherited all the rights and liberties of Englishmen under the common law and the British constitution. Their fifth resolution stated: 'That the respective colonies are entitled to the common law of England, and more especially to the great and inestimable privilege of being

---

[36] Malcolm, 'Magna Carta in America', p. 126.

[37] John Adams's 'Admiralty Notebook', quoted in D. Lovejoy, '"Rights imply equality"', p. 481.

[38] Malcolm, 'Magna Carta in America', p. 126.

[39] Colbourn, *The Lamp of Experience*, p. 164.

tried by their peers of the vicinage, according to the course of that law'.[40] They undoubtedly believed that this claim was based on chapter 29 of the 1225 version of Magna Carta. When South Carolina threw off its allegiance to George III, in early 1776, its chief justice, William Henry Drayton, expressed deep satisfaction that British efforts to abolish the right of trial by jury, in contempt of Magna Carta, would no longer be tolerated under the independent state's new constitution.[41] When, in July 1776, the American colonists finally drafted their Declaration of Independence, their long list of grievances, against the British king, ministers and parliament, included the charges that Britain had used vice-admiralty courts where judicial decisions had been reached without juries and that efforts had been made by Britain to put colonists on trial in courts located far beyond the borders of their provinces.[42]

Far more important than the colonial accusations that Britain was betraying the legal principles enshrined in Magna Carta were the repeated claims made in America that Britain was acting contrary to Magna Carta in maintaining that the Westminster parliament had the right to levy direct internal taxes on the American colonies without the consent of the colonial legislatures. When parliament attempted to levy the Stamp Tax on the colonies, in 1765, the colonists quickly pointed out that consent to taxes must be given by those required to pay them and hence internal taxes levied in America required the consent of local colonial legislatures.[43] They therefore vehemently protested that the Stamp Tax was contrary to the constitutional principle of 'no taxation without representation', a claim very much based on Sir Edward Coke's assertion in the early seventeenth century that Magna Carta had laid down that the crown could only levy taxes with the consent of parliament. On 28 September 1765, the lower house of the Maryland legislative assembly resolved unanimously, 'that it was granted by Magna Charta, ... that the subject should not be compelled to contribute any tax, tallage, aid or other like charge, not set by the common consent of parliament',[44] and hence without the consent of the colonial legislatures. In his resolutions against the Stamp Act presented to the Massachusetts

[40] 'Declaration and Resolves of the First Continental Congress', *The Avalon Project: Documents in Law, History and Diplomacy* <http://avalon.law.yale.edu/18th_century/resolves.asp> [accessed 20 May 2015].

[41] 'Drayton's charge to the Grand Jury of South Carolina, 23 April 1776', in *Principles and Acts of the Revolution in America*, ed. H. Niles (Baltimore, Md., 1822), p. 72.

[42] 'America's Founding Documents', *National Archives* <http://www.archives.gov/exhibits/charters/declaration_transcript.html> [accessed 24 Aug. 2015].

[43] *A Collection of Tracts, on the subjects of taxing the British colonies in America, and regulating their trade* (4 vols., 1773), iii. 105.

[44] *The Proceedings of the North American Colonies in consequence of the Stamp Act* (1766), p. 11; and Morgan, *Prologue to Revolution*, p. 52.

house of representatives, on 29 October 1765, Samuel Adams, a leading Patriot, insisted that a major pillar of the British constitution, to which the colonists could also lay claim, was the principle of no taxation without representation, which 'together with all other essential rights, privileges, and immunities of the people of Great Britain, have been fully confirmed to them by Magna Charta'.[45] The Massachusetts assembly went on to declare that the Stamp Act was invalid because it was 'against Magna Charta and the natural rights of Englishmen, and therefore, according to Lord Coke, null and void'.[46] The New York assembly also insisted in 1765 that no taxation without representation was 'a fundamental principle … declared by Magna Charta'.[47]

Thomas Hutchinson, the lieutenant-governor of Massachusetts, was alarmed at the way local American patriots were exploiting Edward Coke's interpretation of Magna Carta in order to resist the imposition of the Stamp Tax. He declared on 12 September 1765: 'our friends to liberty take the advantage of a maxim they find in Lord Coke that an Act of parliament against Magna Carta or the peculiar rights of Englishmen is *ipso facto* void … This, taken in the latitude the people are often disposed to take it, must be fatal to all government, and it seems to have determined [a] great part of the colony to oppose the execution of the act with force'.[48] The fierce colonial opposition to the Stamp Act was not confined to Massachusetts. Several colonies agreed to send representatives to a Congress in New York in order to co-ordinate their opposition to the Stamp Act. There they resolved that 'The invaluable rights of taxing ourselves … are not, we most humbly conceive Unconstitutional; but confirmed by the great CHARTER of *English Liberty*'.[49] When the Stamp Act was repealed by the Westminster parliament in 1766, Jonathan Mayhew in Boston celebrated this decision on the basis that taxation by consent was a natural right, but it was also a right based on Magna Carta: 'It shall be taken for granted that this natural right is declared, affirmed and secured to us, as we are British subjects, by Magna Charta; all acts contrary to which are said to be *ipso facto* null

---

[45] Quoted in Colbourn, *The Lamp of Experience*, p. 175.

[46] Quoted in *Magna Carta Uncovered*, ed. A. Arlidge and I. Judge (Oxford, 2014), p. 158.

[47] Quoted in J. P. Reid, *Constitutional History of the American Revolution, ii: the Authority to Tax* (Madison, Wis., 1987), p. 108.

[48] Quoted in *Law, Liberty, and Parliament: Selected Essays on the Writings of Sir Edward Coke*, ed. A. D. Boyer (Indianapolis, Ind., 2004), p. 179. See also Hutchinson's comment of 25 Sept. 1765, quoted in Boyer, *Law, Liberty, and Parliament*, p. 180.

[49] *Authentic Account of the Proceedings of the Congress held at New York, in MDCCLXV, on the subject of the American Stamp Act* (New York, 1767), p. 14; and Morgan, *Prologue to Revolution*, p. 65.

and void'.[50] On 27 January 1772, Samuel Adams, now one of the most outspoken of American Patriots, published in the *Boston Gazette* Edward Coke's claim that Magna Carta was 'declaratory of the principal grounds of the fundamental laws and liberties of England'. He added, however, 'whether Lord Coke has expressed it or not ... an act of parliament made against Magna Charta in violation of its essential parts, is void'.[51] In 1775, Moses Mather insisted that the charters of the American colonies were, like Magna Carta, permanent, perpetual and unalterable. He claimed that chapter 29 of Magna Carta established that British subjects, on both sides of the Atlantic, were liable to no taxes and bound by no laws except those made and imposed by their own consent.[52]

The claim that the principle of no taxation without representation was enshrined in Magna Carta was supported by political commentators in America[53] and even by a few in Britain. In July 1768, John Wilkes, a leading pro-American campaigner in London, proclaimed:

> *Liberty* I consider as the birthright of *every* subject of the British empire, and I hold *Magna Charta* to be as full in force in *America* as in *Europe*. I hope that these truths will become generally known and acknowledged through the wide extended dominions of our sovereign, and that a *real union of the whole* will prevail *to save the whole*, and to guard the public liberty, if invaded by despotic ministers, in the most remote, equally as in the central parts of this vast empire.[54]

Shortly before war broke out, James Burgh, a supporter of parliamentary reform in Britain, declared:

> *Magna Charta*, and the Bill of Rights, prohibit the taxing of the mother country by prerogative, and without the consent of those who are to be taxed. If the people of *Britain* are not to be taxed but by parliament; because otherwise they might be taxed without their own consent; does it not directly follow, that the colonists cannot, according to *Magna Charta* and the bill of rights, be taxed by Parliament, so long as they continue unrepresented, because otherwise they may be taxed without their consent.[55]

---

[50] Jonathan Mayhew, *The Snare Broken* (Boston, Mass., 1766), p. 4.

[51] Quoted in Colbourn, *The Lamp of Experience*, p. 175.

[52] Moses Mather, *America's Appeal to the Impartial World* (Hartford, Conn., 1775), pp. 12, 25, 36–7.

[53] See, for example, D. Dulany, *Considerations on the propriety of imposing taxes on the British Colonies for the purpose of raising a revenue, by Act of Parliament* (2nd edn., New York, 1765), p. 31; and [A. Lee,] *An Appeal to the Justice and Interests of the People of Great Britain, in the present disputes with America* (1774), p. 7.

[54] *The Controversial Letters of John Wilkes, Esq, the Rev. John Horne, and their principle* [*sic*] *adherents* (1771), p. 164.

[55] James Burgh, *Political Disquisitions: Or, an enquiry into public errors, defects and abuses* (3 vols., 1774–75), ii. 310.

In an effort to stop the war in its early stages some British supporters of the American cause formed the London Association in 1775.[56] They attacked the British government's determination to use armed force in the colonies and denied that the Americans desired complete independence.[57] To justify their position, they published a pamphlet, in 1776, setting out the most important terms of Magna Carta, complete with Edward Coke's remarks on these.[58] About the same time, another British commentator, who regarded Magna Carta as 'still the impregnable fortress of our privileges', was even more explicit:

> By Magna Charta ... no subject should be compelled to contribute any tax ... not set by the common consent of Parliament. Our colonists are subjects of the British dominions. In the parliament of Great Britain, which is only a part of those dominions, they are not represented. The imposition, therefore, of any tax, by that Parliament, must be without the consent of the colonists; and it follows that they are absolutely exempted from the necessity of submitting to it.[59]

On both sides of the Atlantic, however, American Patriots and British radicals began to rely more on the belief that their political rights and liberties were better defended by appeals to fundamental law[60] and natural rights than by Magna Carta. James Otis[61] and James Wilson,[62] for example, maintained that English liberties had existed long before Magna Carta and that the great charter had merely declared what had long been regarded as natural rights and fundamental law in England. In 1767, Silas Downer of Providence, Rhode Island declared of the doctrine of no taxation without

---

[56] J. Sainsbury, *Disaffected Patriots: London Supporters of Revolutionary America 1769–1782* (Kingston and Montreal, and Gloucester, 1987), pp. 106–13, 118.

[57] The 'Circular Letter from the London Association' and 'Resolutions of the London Association', in *The Crisis*, lxxxviii, pp. 554–6 and the 'Prefatory Address from the London association' printed in *The Declaration by the Representatives of the United Colonies of North America, now met in general congress at Philadelphia, setting forth the causes and necessity of taking up arms* (1775), pp. iii–vi.

[58] *The Golden Passage in the Great Charter of England, called Magna Charta ... with Lord Coke's Remarks and Explanations. Printed for the Use of the London Association* (1776).

[59] *Taxation, Tyranny. Addressed to Samuel Johnson* (1775), pp. 26–7. Samuel Johnson had recently published a pamphlet, *Taxation No Tyranny*, which supported the right of the Westminster parliament to tax the American colonies.

[60] J. P. Reid, '"In our Contracted Sphere": the constitutional contract, the Stamp Act crisis, and the coming of the American Revolution', *Columbia Law Rev.*, lxxxvi (1976), 21–47; and T. C. Grey, 'Origins of the unwritten constitution: fundamental law in American revolutionary thought', *Stanford Law Rev.*, xxx (1978), 843–93.

[61] James Otis, *The Rights of the British Colonies Asserted and Proven* (Boston, 1764), p. 31.

[62] Colbourn, *The Lamp of Experience*, p. 126.

representation that: 'It is a natural right which no creature can *give*, or hath a right to take away. The great charter of liberties, commonly called Magna Charta, doth not *give* the privileges therein mentioned, nor doth our *Charters*, but must be considered as only declaratory of our rights, and in affirmance of them'.[63] Samuel Langdon, president of Harvard College, proclaimed in a sermon preached in 1775, 'Thanks be to God that He has given us, as men, natural rights, independent of all human laws whatsoever, and that these rights are recognized by the grand charter of English liberties'.[64] William Gordon went so far as to claim that Magna Carta provided no solid security for the rights and liberties of the British or the American people when parliament could amend or ignore its terms by passing statute laws.[65]

As the American crisis developed, however, these concerns did not prevent appeals being made to Magna Carta in order to justify using force to oppose the British government and parliament, both of which were increasingly regarded by the American colonists as arbitrary and oppressive. As early as November 1772, some Boston Patriots declared that Magna Carta 'was justly obtain'd of King John sword in hand: and peradventure it must one day sword in hand again be rescued and preserv'd from total destruction and oblivion'.[66] In 'The Forester's Letters', Thomas Paine defended the natural rights of the colonists and denied Magna Carta had created any new rights, but he did concede that 1215 had shown how a king could be forced to renounce tyranny.[67] Charles Carroll also stressed that Magna Carta had been achieved by force,[68] while John Adams used the events of 1215 to claim: 'Did not the English gain by resistance to John, when Magna Charta was obtained'.[69] In 'A Pastoral Letter', of 1775, four Presbyterian ministers in Pennsylvania advised their co-religionists in North Carolina that: 'To take any man's money, without his consent is unjust and contrary to reason and the law of God … it is contrary to Magna Charta, or the Great Charter and Constitution of England; and to complain, and even to resist such a lawless power, is just and reasonable, and no rebellion'.[70] At a provincial convention in Philadelphia, in January 1775, James Wilson claimed that the

---

[63] Quoted by Malcolm, 'Magna Carta in America', p. 129.
[64] Quoted in Dick Howard, *The Road from Runnymede*, p. 185.
[65] Dick Howard, *The Road from Runnymede*, p. 184.
[66] *The Votes and Proceedings of the Freeholders and other Inhabitants of the Town of Boston, in town meetings assembled, according to law* (Boston, Mass., 1772), p. 8.
[67] Malcolm, 'Magna Carta in America', p. 129.
[68] Colbourn, *The Lamp of Experience*, p. 141.
[69] Quoted in Colbourn, *The Lamp of Experience*, p. 92.
[70] Quoted in J. C. D. Clark, *The Language of Liberty 1660–1832: Political Discourse and Social Dynamics in the Anglo-American World* (Cambridge, 1994), p. 360.

armed resistance now being contemplated by the American colonists was the same as the barons had used in securing Magna Carta in 1215. In his view, the right of resistance was founded on both the letter and the spirit of the British constitution.[71] When some colonial representatives at the second Continental Congress, held in Philadelphia in 1776, questioned the legitimacy of taking up arms against King George III, Wilson pointed out that such an objection had not prevented the English barons from resisting the tyranny of King John in 1215 and gaining the concessions he agreed to in Magna Carta.[72]

When the American colonists finally took up arms to secure their independence from Britain they began creating new state constitutions for their provinces. In drafting written constitutions, they hoped to create fundamental laws, which could not so easily be amended or revoked by a sovereign legislature as had happened in Britain in recent decades. Many colonies, including Virginia, Maryland, Delaware, North Carolina and South Carolina in 1776, New York in 1777, Massachusetts in 1780, and New Hampshire in 1784, incorporated in their new constitutions the essential features of chapter 29 of the 1225 version of Magna Carta.[73] The Virginia Bill of Rights of 1776 declared that an accused person should receive a speedy trial before an impartial jury in the locality where the offence had occurred, that 'no man could be deprived of his liberty, except by the law of the land or the judgment of his peers', and that no excessive fines should be imposed nor cruel or unusual punishments inflicted.[74] Several states explicitly guaranteed that 'no person shall be deprived of life, liberty, or property, without due process of law', that any accused person must be tried by the law of the land and by a jury of his peers in the vicinity where the offence took place, and that justice should not be sold, denied or delayed.[75] In Massachusetts in 1779, John Adams declared that any government seeking to serve the public interest must be a government of laws not of men. In England, Magna Carta had been an attempt to serve such a purpose, but its specific terms and general principles had been frequently broken by king or parliament and the people had often been forced to repair the damage

[71] Colbourn, *The Lamp of Experience*, p. 123.

[72] *An Address to the Inhabitants of the Colonies* (1776) in *The Collected Works of James Wilson*, ed. K. L. Hall and M. D. Hall (2 vols., Indianapolis, Ind., 2007), i. 49.

[73] *Magna Carta and its Modern Legacy*, ed. R. Hazell and J. Melton (Cambridge, 2015), pp. 9 and 83; and H. D. Hazeltine, 'The influence of Magna Carta on American constitutional development', *Columbia Law Rev.*, xvii (1917), 1–33, at pp. 25–6.

[74] Niles, *Principles and Acts of the Revolution in America*, pp. 123–4; and Magraw et al., *Magna Carta and the Rule of Law*, ed. Magraw *et al.*, p. 161.

[75] Malcolm, 'Magna Carta in America', pp. 131–2; and Dick Howard, *The Road from Runnymede*, pp. 204–13.

done to their rights and liberties. The American colonies now fighting for their independence must try to avoid such a fate by clearly stating their rights and liberties, and limiting the powers of their legislatures in their new written constitutions.[76] Adams helped ensure that the Massachusetts constitution of 1780 included no less than three articles, which could be traced back to the terms of Magna Carta.[77]

After securing their independence in 1783 the new American states recognized the need to establish a more effective national government than they had managed to achieve during the War of Independence. In the debates on establishing a new Federal Constitution that took place in 1787 in Philadelphia, there was little discussion among the representatives about how it might be influenced by the terms and principles of Magna Carta. James Wilson even pointed out that the Americans no longer had any need to look back to Magna Carta for inspiration because that charter of rights and liberties had been granted to the English people by their monarch, whereas the United States was a republic in which the people were establishing their own rights by their own efforts. In his view, the American people would retain all the rights and liberties not explicitly surrendered in their new Federal Constitution.[78] The terms of the Federal Constitution were drafted in 1787, but it was then sent out in 1788 for ratification by the states. This process, which lasted some months, led to disputes between Federalists and Anti-Federalists about whether the new constitution had done enough to protect the rights and liberties of individuals. Although it has been suggested that there was little discussion of Magna Carta by those chosen to ratify the constitution,[79] there was in fact some discussion of its relevance by major commentators on the issues at stake. The leading Federalists, James Madison and Alexander Hamilton, shared James Wilson's view that there was no need to include specific guarantees for the rights of the individual in the terms of the Federal Constitution. They maintained that whereas Magna Carta had been needed by the English people to secure their rights and liberties against an arbitrary and oppressive monarch, in America's new republic there was no need to guarantee the rights of the individual since the powers of the Federal legislature and the elected

[76] W. F. Swindler, *Magna Carta: Legend and Legacy* (New York, 1965), p. 228.

[77] Dick Howard, *The Road from Runnymede*, pp. 209–11.

[78] Dick Howard, *The Road from Runnymede*, p. 225; and J. N. Rakove, *Original Meanings: Politics and Ideas in the Making of the Constitution* (New York, 1996), p. 326. Wilson's view was commended in Alexander Contee Hanson, *Remarks on the proposed plan of a federal government, addressed to the citizens of the United States of America, and particularly to the people of Maryland* (Annapolis, Md., 1788), p. 27.

[79] P. Maier, *Ratification: the Public Debate on the Constitution 1787–1788* (New York, 2010).

president were clearly limited by the express terms of the new constitution. In *The Federalist Papers*, Alexander Hamilton specifically mentioned that there was no need to emulate the English people in securing a Magna Carta style charter of liberties. Such a charter could 'have no application to constitutions founded [like the Federal Constitution] upon the power of the people, and executed by their immediate representatives and servants. Here, in strictness, the people surrender nothing; as they retain every thing they have no need of particular reservations ... here is a better recognition of popular rights'.[80] Madison claimed that the English people's 'Magna Charta does not contain one provision for the security of these rights, respecting which the people of America are most alarmed. The freedom of the press and rights of conscience, those choicest privileges of the people, are unguarded in the British constitution'.[81] James Iredell and Samuel Johnston both opposed the demand for a specific Bill of Rights to be added to the Federal Constitution because the evidence of British history showed that a sovereign legislature there had possessed the authority to alter or revoke various parts of Magna Carta.[82] Governor Johnston asked those at the North Carolina Convention, 'What is Magna Charta? It is only an act of Parliament. Their Parliament can, at any time, alter the whole, or any part of it. It is no more binding on the people than any other law Parliament has passed'.[83] In the new American republic, by contrast, the powers of the American Congress were clearly circumscribed by the terms of the Federal Constitution. David Ramsay, one of the first historians of the American Revolution, made this distinction crystal clear in an oration celebrating the anniversary of the Declaration of Independence in 1794. While willing to accept that Magna Carta had been freely granted to the English people by their king, he nevertheless concluded,

> What is said to be thus given and granted by the free will of the sovereign, we, the people of America, hold in our own right. The sovereignty rests in ourselves, and instead of receiving the privileges of free citizens as a boon from the hands of our rulers, we defined their powers by a constitution of our own framing, which prescribed to them, that this far they might go, but no farther. All power, not thus expressly delegated, is retained.[84]

---

[80] Alexander Hamilton, 'Certain general and miscellaneous objections to the constitution considered and answered', *The Federalist Papers*, lxxxiv (July–Aug. 1788).

[81] Quoted in Dick Howard, *The Road from Runnymede*, p. 234.

[82] Dick Howard, *The Road from Runnymede*, pp. 230–1.

[83] *Proceedings and debates of the Convention of North-Carolina ... for the purpose of deliberating and determining the Constitution* (Edenton, N.C., 1789), p. 86.

[84] David Ramsay, *An Oration, delivered on the anniversary of American independence, July 4, 1794 ... to the inhabitants of Charleston* (1795), p. 18.

Despite such efforts, Anti-Federalists remained seriously concerned about the absence of any mention in the Federal Constitution of the rights and liberties of the individual. They maintained that Magna Carta had indeed provided an important security for the rights and liberties of Englishmen and they wished to see something similar included in the new constitution before it was fully ratified.[85] Representatives from Virginia, for example, put forward the view that the Federal Constitution needed to be amended to ensure that such rights and liberties as had been protected in England by Magna Carta would be secured in the new republic. They urged that no accused person should be punished except by due process, according to the law of the land; that justice should neither be delayed nor denied; and that an accused person should be given a fair and speedy trial before a jury drawn from the area where the offence had been committed.[86] These were all civil rights, which the Americans had long believed were enshrined in chapter 29 of the 1225 version of Magna Carta.

In the event, Congress decided to give way to the demands of the Anti-Federalists. In 1791, a Bill of Rights, proposed by the leading Federalist, James Madison, added ten amendments to the Federal Constitution.[87] Several of these amendments were clearly influenced by some of the most famous and cherished terms of Magna Carta. The First Amendment guaranteed citizens the right to petition for the redress of grievances. The Fifth Amendment declared that 'No person shall be ... deprived of life, liberty, or property, without due process of law; nor shall private property be taken for public use, without just compensation'. This clearly owed much to chapter 29 of the 1225 version of Magna Carta. The Sixth Amendment, also clearly influenced by Magna Carta, provided that 'the accused shall enjoy the right of a speedy and public trial, by an impartial jury of the State and district wherein the crime shall have been committed'. The Seventh Amendment established jury trials in civil cases and the Eighth Amendment prohibited cruel and unusual punishments; both of which were influenced by Magna Carta, through earlier English statutes and American state constitutions.[88] In the early years of the republic (and long afterwards) appeals were made to Magna Carta a great many times

[85] Hazell and Melton, *Magna Carta and its Modern Legacy*, p. 13.
[86] Dick Howard, *The Road from Runnymede*, pp. 232–3.
[87] G. S. Wood, 'The origins of the Bill of Rights', *Proc. American Antiquarian Soc.*, ci (1991), 255–74.
[88] Hazell and Melton, *Magna Carta and its Modern Legacy*, pp. 10–11; and *Magna Carta, Religion and the Rule of Law*, ed. R. Griffith-Jones and M. Hill (Cambridge, 2015), pp. 93–6 and 139.

by American lawyers pleading their cases before both state and federal courts.[89]

Before and during the War of Independence a number of American Patriots had used the example of the English barons using force to compel King John to accept the terms of Magna Carta to justify their own resort to arms against what they regarded as Britain's oppressive and arbitrary policies adopted since the early 1760s. Before and during the drafting of the Federal Constitution a number of Americans commented on the difficulties that the English had had in securing the rights and liberties which they believed that they had been granted by means of Magna Carta. The Americans were aware that an effort had been made in chapter 61 of the original Magna Carta of 1215 to ensure that King John would observe the terms in the Charter to which he had given his consent. In this chapter the rebellious barons had proposed electing representatives from within their ranks, who could determine whether an appeal to arms needed to be made in order to ensure that King John fulfilled his obligations under the terms set out in Magna Carta. The Americans knew, however, that this chapter had been omitted from all subsequent versions and confirmations of Magna Carta. No mechanism therefore had ever been established to ensure that the terms of Magna Carta could be enforced. The Americans soon found a means by which the authority of the executive and legislature created by the Federal Constitution could be effectively prevented from exceeding the powers granted to them by the terms of this constitution. A supreme court was established quite independent of the executive and the legislature. The justices of the supreme court soon established their power of judicial review. They took it upon themselves to adjudicate whether any action by the executive or the legislature in the United States could be judged as exceeding the powers granted to these institutions by the Federal Constitution. In 1803, in the case of *Marbury v. Madison*, Chief Justice John Marshall used the arguments previously used by Edward Coke in England in the early seventeenth century to assert that the supreme court had the right to declare some executive or legislative actions to be unconstitutional.[90] The principle and practice of judicial review became an extremely important, if often contested, aspect of the American Constitution.[91] When the supreme court was housed in its fine building in Washington D.C. it was therefore appropriate that its magnificent bronze doors included among their eight

[89] Magraw *et al.*, *Magna Carta and the Rule of Law*, pp. 70–3, 94–6; H. D. Hazeltine, 'The influence of Magna Carta on American constitutional development', *Columbia Law Review*, xvii (1917), 1–33, at pp. 26–33; Malcolm, 'Magna Carta in America', p. 135.

[90] Dick Howard, *The Road from Runnymede*, pp. 276–80.

[91] Magraw *et al.*, *Magna Carta and the Rule of Law*, pp. 111–140.

panels, an image of King John agreeing to Magna Carta at Runnymede in 1215, another of King Edward I confirming Magna Carta in 1297, and a third showing Sir Edward Coke disputing with King James I.

8. Reform, radicalism and revolution: Magna Carta in eighteenth- and nineteenth-century Britain*

Alexander Lock

Throughout the eighteenth and nineteenth centuries Magna Carta was invoked extensively across Great Britain and its empire. Building on the foundations laid in the seventeenth century it had become a document of international scope and influence as vigorously debated by radicals in Westminster as by lawyers in Bengal or rebels in Massachusetts.[1] Throughout the period Magna Carta was used to champion press freedom and parliamentary reform, to challenge transportation and naval impressment, and in debates to regulate overseas trade and taxation.[2] The range of media on which its image was reproduced was as broad and unusual as the principles and people it was engaged to defend. In the age of the industrial revolution its image was reproduced and sold on statuary, playing cards, fabrics, prints, porcelain and paintings; bought by an increasing pool of consumers eager

---

* Note to the reader: unless otherwise stated, all clauses cited in this essay relate to the Great Charter sealed by King John in 1215. Small parts of this essay have previously appeared in print as 'Radicalism and reform', in *Magna Carta: Law, Liberty, Legacy*, ed. C. Breay and J. Harrison (2015), pp. 161–6. The use of Magna Carta by parliamentary reformers is the subject of this essay, but, for further discussion of the subject, see also A. Pallister, *Magna Carta: the Heritage of Liberty* (Oxford, 1971), pp. 59–75.

[1] For its invocation by British subjects in Bengal, see British Library, India Office Records, IOR/H/144, 'The Humble Petition of the British Subjects Residing in the Province of Bengal, Behar, and Orissa and their Several Dependencies', 26 Feb. 1779; *Observations on the Foregoing Petition of the British Subjects Residing in Bengal* (1779), p. 37. For its invocation by revolutionaries in North America see A. E. Dick Howard, *The Road from Runnymede: Magna Carta and Constitutionalism in America* (Charlottesville, Va., 1968), pp. 133–240.

[2] On press freedom, see below in this essay and R. V. Turner, *Magna Carta through the Ages* (2003), pp. 176–7. For an example of the uses of Magna Carta to challenge transportation and naval impressment, see J. Bentham, *A Plea for the Constitution* (1803), pp. 16–19, 55–7; J. E. Oglethorpe, *The Sailor's Advocate* (1728); *The Case of The King Against Alexander Broadfoot, at the Session of Oyer and Terminer and Goal Delivery Held for the City of Bristol and County of the Same City, on 30 of August, 1743* (Oxford, 1758), pp. 3, 25–26; Nauticus, *The Rights of the Sailors Vindicated* (1772), pp. vi-vii, xiii, 20. For its use in contemporary debates on overseas trade, see *An Essay towards a Scheme or Model for Erecting a National East-India Joynt-Stock or Company* (1691), p. 6.

A. Lock, 'Reform, radicalism and revolution: Magna Carta in eighteenth- and nineteenth-century Britain', in *Magna Carta: history, context and influence*, ed. L. Goldman (2018), pp. 101–16.

to own something of Britain's glorious heritage.[3] Just as their seventeenth-century predecessors had done, radicals and revolutionaries continued to employ the Great Charter in order to embarrass the monarch, promote political reform and, if necessary, foment insurrection. However, where once Magna Carta was enlisted by parliament in their struggle for supremacy over the crown, the eighteenth- and nineteenth-centuries' reformers used it to challenge the very authority and power that (the unrepresentative) parliament had won.[4]

Yet for all these invocations Magna Carta was rarely read by those who used it and barely understood in its historical context. It had become little more than a heroic symbol of 'English liberty', the embodiment of an unwritten and reputedly ancient constitution. Citations of the Great Charter tended to be crude and anachronistic and beyond the general defence of due process famously given in chapters 39 and 40 (that 'No freeman will be taken or imprisoned or disseised or outlawed or exiled or in anyway ruined ... save by the lawful judgement of his peers or by the law of the land. To no one shall we sell, to no one shall we deny or delay right or justice') its advocates were less concerned with its specific clauses than with its iconographical significance. Magna Carta had become a slogan calculated to stir patriotic emotions and mobilize public support.

When discussing the history of Magna Carta and the 'rights' contained within it, eighteenth- and nineteenth-century commentators frequently used the terms 'Englishmen' and 'Britons' interchangeably. Many who did so were simply indulging in 'the nasty English habit' of using the words synonymously, while others tacitly suggested that the 'rights' contained within England's Magna Carta appealed to and were legitimately claimed by most British subjects.[5] As Colin Kidd has noted, 'English liberties

---

[3] For examples of this material, see Breay and Harrison, *Magna Carta: Law, Liberty, Legacy*, pp. 168–89.

[4] Pallister, *Magna Carta: the Heritage of Liberty*, pp. 43–75.

[5] K. Kumar, *The Making of English National Identity* (Cambridge, 2003), p. 275, n. 6. Though beyond the scope of this essay, the suggestion that such rights could be legitimately claimed by all British subjects engendered contentious discussions within the British empire. Whilst the jurisdiction of 'English liberties' remained a contested issue well into the 20th century, one recurring feature of the debates was the suggestion that such rights were 'inherited' in the colonies along racial lines (see M. Taylor, 'Magna Carta in the nineteenth century', in *Magna Carta: the Foundation of Freedom, 1215–2015*, ed. N. Vincent (2014), pp. 136–53, at pp. 150–3; *Exclusionary Empire: English Liberty Overseas, 1600–1900*, ed. J. P. Greene (Cambridge, 2010), pp. 55, 66, 193, 228; *Australia's Empire*, ed. D. M. Schreuder and S. Ward (Oxford, 2009), p. 21; D. O'Brien, 'Magna Carta, the "sugar colonies" and "fantasies of empire"', in *Magna Carta and its Modern Legacy*, ed. R. Hazell and J. Melton (Cambridge, 2015), pp. 99–122).

embodied universal aspirations to freedom and self-government' that were attractive to the wider British world where there was 'a strong identification with the values and institutions of the English motherland'.[6] Protestant Irish and colonial Americans claimed themselves to be of 'English stock' and 'heirs to the precious English liberties of their Anglo-Saxon ancestors', while their Welsh and Scottish compatriots perceived union with England entitled them to such rights.[7] In this context, to describe Magna Carta as the 'birthright' and 'inheritance' of both 'Englishmen' and 'Britons' was perfectly acceptable.[8] Indeed, as we shall see, even where protest against English domination took place, given the commanding role of England within Britain and its colonial possessions, it is unsurprising that such opposition was often couched in the language of English legal traditions such as Magna Carta and habeas corpus.[9]

The powerful public authority that Magna Carta had achieved as a symbolic document in the eighteenth and nineteenth centuries is evident in its almost ubiquitous visual representation in political cartoons and caricatures of the period. And it was not only those who opposed the government that invoked it. As in the seventeenth century, the Great Charter remained a protean document in the eighteenth and nineteenth centuries, its malleability exploited to advocate a range of political perspectives. Loyalist propagandists claimed that only a strong monarch and elite parliament could defend the 'constitution' and 'principles' of 1215, while at the same time their radical opponents seeking parliamentary reform insisted that the government's grip on power contravened the legal 'birthright' and 'inheritance' of the people's 'ancient' liberties.[10]

[6] C. Kidd, 'Integration: patriotism and nationalism', in *A Companion to Eighteenth Century Britain*, ed. H. Dickinson (Oxford, 2002), pp. 369–80, at p. 376. See also C. Kidd, 'North Britishness and the nature of eighteenth-century British patriotisms', *Hist. Jour.*, xxxix (1996), 361–82; Kumar, *The Making of English National Identity*, pp. 154–6.

[7] Kidd, 'Integration', p. 376.

[8] One of the most striking contemporary pamphlets to claim Magna Carta was 'the Glory of Britain and Ireland' (see H. Hone and G. Cruikshank, *The Queen and Magna Charta; Or, the Thing that John Signed* (1820)). Throughout, it consciously depicted Scots, Irish and English altogether celebrating 'the thing that John signed'.

[9] Kumar, *The Making of English National Identity*, p. 156. In Ireland the Irish nationalist and political writer Wolfe Tone (1763–98) invoked Magna Carta regarding Catholic rights in Ireland, while American colonists in the decade leading up to, and during, the America War of Independence readily looked to the Great Charter to support their claims against the actions of the British government (see *The Writings of Theobald Wolfe Tone 1763–98*, ed. T. W. Moody, R. B. McDowell and C. J. Woods (3 vols., Oxford, 2007), i. 177; Turner, *Magna Carta through the Ages*, pp. 212–17).

[10] W. Cobbett, 'A letter to the freemen of the city of Coventry, 4 April 1818', *Cobbett's Weekly Political Register*, xxx (1818), cols. 379–410, esp. cols. 381–2.

Yet, for all their political contestation, the constitutional iconography of these popular prints, both loyalist and radical alike, was straightforward: the legitimate political actors defended the Charter from destruction or desecration, while the tyrannical and illegitimate trampled it underfoot, lost, tore, or stabbed it.[11] By the eighteenth century, these representations of the Charter were combined with a canon of other symbolic achievements – habeas corpus, the Phrygian (or Liberty) Cap of antiquity, the Constitution, the Bill of Rights (1688) – which were little engaged with as things in themselves but in combination represented the liberties of freeborn Britons whose public reverence lent the semblance of political legitimacy. William Hone's (1780–1842) pro-reform poem *The Political House that Jack Built* (1819) and M. Adams' loyalist response *A Parody on the Political House that Jack Built* (1820) vividly demonstrate how these rich political symbols could be used by contested groups. Both authors agreed that Magna Carta, the Bill of Rights and habeas corpus constituted 'the WEALTH that lays In the House that Jack Built', but fundamentally disagreed as to how this inheritance was to be best preserved. For the radical Hone, the unrepresentative, plutocratic parliamentarians and sycophantic soldiery, placemen, and privy councillors represented the greatest threat, while for the loyalist Adams it was 'THE VERMIN' reformer 'who despises all Laws' that would irrevocably 'injure' this 'Wealth, That Lays in the House, That Jack Built'.[12] Notably, neither Hone nor Adams explored the details of Magna Carta's history or how it would be undermined by their opponents. Its image was only used as it presented an easily recognizable ideogram for 'constitutional rights'.

While Magna Carta would become an important symbol for parliamentary reformers in the later eighteenth century, it was in the decades immediately following the Glorious Revolution (1688) that the framework was established in which Magna Carta would emerge as an integral part of reformist propaganda.[13] Following the jurisprudence of the late Elizabethan and early Stuart lawyer Sir Edward Coke (1552–1634), the predominant seventeenth-century interpretation of Magna Carta was that it reaffirmed the ancient immemorial rights and liberties of the English and formed the basis of a fundamental, unalterable, law.[14] However, the Revolution Settlement that

[11] For a description of the numerous prints, see M. D. George, *English Political Caricature 1793–1832: a Study of Opinion and Propaganda* (2 vols., Oxford, 1959), i. 44, 54, 60, 69, 83, 95, 125, 126, 132, 137, 144, 146, 157, 182, 195, 199; i. 13, 23, 81, 125, 126, 175, 181.

[12] W. Hone, *The Political House that Jack Built* (1819), *passim*; M. Adams, *A Parody on the Political House that Jack Built: or the Real House that Jack Built* (1820), pp. 2–3.

[13] Pallister, *Magna Carta: the Heritage of Liberty*, p. 42.

[14] F. Thompson, *Magna Carta: its Role in the Making of the English Constitution, 1300–1629* (1948), pp. 354–75; S. D. White, *Sir Edward Coke and the Grievances of the Commonwealth*

restricted the power of the monarchy and vested sovereignty with parliament following the Glorious Revolution eventually, and unwittingly, challenged this long-held narrative by undermining the supposed independence vested in these 'ancient' immemorial laws. Parliament had become the state's supreme law-making body whose capacity to enact, amend and repeal law (including clauses from Magna Carta) weakened the authority of the Great Charter as an ancient, immutable, law. The Bill of Rights (1689), a document that was ironically claimed as 'our second *Magna Charta*' by Viscount Bolingbroke (1678–1751), placed Magna Carta's former guardian, parliament, in the ascendancy and so supplanted the Great Charter as the immemorial bulwark of English liberties.[15]

Yet, Magna Carta endured and became an important instrument in political debates about the capacity of parliament to alter fundamental laws. As Anne Pallister has argued, once 'the implications of the Revolution Settlement to individual liberty became obvious, the Charter once more re-emerged as ... a weapon to be used against the new tyranny of a class-dominated sovereign parliament'.[16] Magna Carta was raised in this regard in 1701, following the imprisonment by parliament of five Kentish petitioners who had presented a series of policy demands to the house of commons and asked that the Members 'have regard to the voice of the people'.[17] Their imprisonment made clear the capacity for parliament to act as arbitrarily as any monarch, prompting the publication of a range of anti-government pamphlets. The lawyer and whig politician John Somers (1651–1716) argued in his *Jura Populi Anglicani* (1701) that imprisoning the Kentish petitioners 'was repugnant to *Magna Charta* ... and all the other Acts which designed to secure our Liberties from the Invasion of our Kings' leaving the public 'expos'd to the Arbitrary Will of our *Fellow Commoners*'.[18] The novelist Daniel Defoe (1660?–1731) similarly responded, presenting his 'Legions Memorial' to the speaker of the house of commons, Robert Harley (1661–1724), in which he urged the petitioners' to be released exhorting that 'Englishmen are no more to be Slaves to Parliaments than to Kings'[19]

(Manchester, 1979), pp. 245–70.

[15] H. St. John, Viscount Bolingbroke, *A Collection of Political Tracts* (1748), p. 246; Turner, *Magna Carta through the Ages*, p. 171.

[16] Pallister, *Magna Carta: the Heritage of Liberty*, p. 42.

[17] M. Goldie, 'The English system of liberty', in *The Cambridge History of Eighteenth-Century Political Thought*, ed. M. Goldie and R. Wokler (Cambridge, 2006), pp. 40–78, at p. 61.

[18] J. Somers, Baron Somers, *Jura Populi Anglicani: Or, the Subjects Right of Petitioning Set Forth* (1701), p. 17.

[19] W. Cobbett, *The Parliamentary History of England from the Earliest Period to the Year 1803* (36 vols., 1811), v. 1256.

The Great Charter and the rights of the subject were similarly invoked in 1716 by opponents to the Septennial Act (1 Geo. I, st. 2, c. 38) which increased the maximum length a parliament could sit from three to seven years. Stressing what he believed to be the contractual nature of parliamentary authority Archibald Hutcheson (1659?–1740), M.P. for Hastings, described the Bill as 'a very dangerous step towards the undermining of that constitution which our ancestors have been so careful to preserve'.[20] Passing it, Hutcheson argued, would equate to giving 'up the Habeas Corpus act, and all the other privileges and immunities, which have been obtained to the people ... from the date of Magna Charta to this very day'.[21] For these men, clearly, parliament was to be limited by the ancient laws and liberties of the people; yet in practice, many also recognized that despite Coke's contentions to the contrary, no government, however undesirable, could govern effectively if it was bound by the actions of their predecessors and no law, however 'ancient', was immutable. As the poet Jonathan Swift (1667–1745) noted in 1710 in the tory newspaper *The Examiner*:

> ... in every Government ... there is placed a supream, absolute, unlimited Power ... [and] wherever is entrusted the Power of making Laws, that Power is without all Bounds; can repeal or enact at Pleasure whatever Laws it thinks fit ... agreeable to our old Constitution; yet at the same Time they allow it to be defeasible by Act of Parliament; and so is Magna Charta too, if the Legislature think fit; which is a Truth so manifest, that no Man who understands the Nature of Government, can be in doubt concerning it.[22]

Such recognition of parliament's growing sovereignty and the dichotomy this presented about the needs of an effective government at the expense of the 'ancient rights' of the subject led to wide-ranging discussions in the early eighteenth century regarding the mutability of the Great Charter and the ancient constitution it had come to represent.[23] It was these debates that first led the noted jurist and judge Sir William Blackstone (1723–80) to Magna Carta in his *The Great Charter and the Charter of the Forest* (1759).[24] A pioneering piece of historical scholarship, based on an examination of the original documents, Blackstone's *The Great Charter* for the first time drew a proper distinction between the Magna Carta of 1215 and its subsequent reissues. It contained transcriptions of the various issues of Magna Carta

---

[20] Cobbett, *The Parliamentary History of England*, vii. 339.

[21] Cobbett, *The Parliamentary History of England*, vii. 347.

[22] *The Examiner*, no. 33, 22 March 1710, in Jonathan Swift, *The works of the Reverend Dr. Jonathan Swift* (20 vols., Dublin, 1772), v. 320–2.

[23] See Pallister, *Magna Carta: the Heritage of Liberty*, pp. 43–58.

[24] N. Vincent, *Magna Carta: a Very Short Introduction* (Oxford, 2012), pp. 97–8.

alongside other key medieval documents that traced the history of Magna Carta from the Articles of the Barons of 1215 to the confirmation of the Charter by Edward I in 1300.[25] In so doing Blackstone demonstrated categorically that Magna Carta had evolved as a legal document between 1215 and 1300 and as such was far from representing a fixed, fundamental, unalterable law. Magna Carta, it would seem, had been eclipsed and parliament's sovereignty fully established.[26]

Yet, Magna Carta was not overshadowed for long and by the mid eighteenth century it once again re-emerged as an important symbol integral to propaganda challenging the arbitrary actions of parliament.[27] Unsurprisingly, the actual, and rather problematic, history of Magna Carta was entirely ignored in this propaganda in which the Great Charter emerged as a simple symbol representing the liberties of freeborn Englishmen over which the government carelessly rode rough shod. Though it was widely used throughout the early eighteenth century to challenge the government during the Excise Crisis (1733) and to oppose naval impressment (which was represented as a violation of clause 39), it was the radical politician and newspaper editor John Wilkes (1725–97) who capitalized most successfully upon the Charter to mobilize public opinion in his favour following his arrest under a General Warrant in 1763.[28]

Wilkes was arrested for libelling King George III (r. 1760–1820) in the infamous number 45 issue of his newspaper the *North Briton* and his subsequent struggles against the government for his own liberty, press freedom (against General Warrants) and ultimate election to parliament and the mayoralty of London all shamelessly exploited the symbol of Magna Carta to great effect achieving widespread – and at times violent – public support.[29] Wilkes was a master propagandist who utilized the symbolism of the Great Charter to represent his causes as ones of national importance regarding the rights of freeborn Britons whose liberties – as he argued his arrest had proven – were under threat. Under Wilkes, Magna Carta became an ideograph that represented a form of ancient liberty, the 'birthright of every subject', which the government under Lord Bute (1713–92) and

---

[25] R. Sweet, *Antiquaries: the Discovery of the Past in Eighteenth-Century Britain* (2004), pp. 234–5, 280; Breay and Harrison, *Magna Carta: Law, Liberty, Legacy*, p. 169.

[26] William Blackstone, *The Great Charter and Charter of the Forest* (Oxford, 1759), *passim*.

[27] Pallister, *Magna Carta: the Heritage of Liberty*, pp. 59–75.

[28] British Museum, Department of Prints and Drawings, 1868,0808.3563, *Excise in Triumph* (1733); Oglethorpe, *The Sailor's Advocate*, pp. 4–5; *The Case of The King Against Alexander Broadfoot*, pp. 3, 25–6; Turner, *Magna Carta through the Ages*, pp. 176–7, 179.

[29] For the events surrounding Wilkes's arrest see, P. D. G. Thomas, *John Wilkes: a Friend to Liberty* (Oxford, 1996), pp. 27–56.

George III were undermining with their General Warrants and backstairs conniving.[30]

Wilkes, who by 1764 had been forced into exile in Paris, never lost an opportunity to appear with Magna Carta in popular propaganda, most notably on cheap political handbills and broadsides, in popular prints and on grand private portraits.[31] In this he was consciously copying a tradition well established by the seventeenth-century polemicist John Lilburne (1614–57), whose name was inextricably connected with Magna Carta and freedom of the press.[32] The two were frequently compared by eighteenth-century commentators and their resemblance was so keenly felt that Wilkes was presented with a Lilburne medal and copy of Theodorus Verax's *The Triall of Lieut. Colonell John Lilburne* (1649) by supporters following his arrest in 1763.[33]

Enterprising businessmen seeking to profit from Wilkes's popularity equally enhanced the Wilkite association with the Great Charter producing porcelain figurines, plates, jugs and teapots for the popular market depicting Wilkes, charter in hand.[34] Even the illustrious manufactory Wedgwood at Etruria in Staffordshire produced highly desirable wares depicting Wilkes with Magna Carta for their wealthy customers, the designs for which were again copied and sold by less prestigious potteries to lower middling clients keen to celebrate their hero Wilkes.[35] The fact that manufacturers went to such lengths demonstrates the popularity of both the document, and Wilkes, and the success he achieved in combining his causes with the idea of English liberty represented in the form of the Great Charter.

A similar example of the potency of Magna Carta as a visual invocation of national political legitimacy and liberty in the eighteenth century can be seen in the episode prompted by the arrest, in November 1762, of Arthur

---

[30] Thomas, *John Wilkes: a Friend to Liberty*, p. 161.

[31] For some of the many examples of this material, see Brit. Museum, 1887,0307,II.46, 'Porcelain Figurine of John Wilkes', Derby, *c*.1768; Brit. Museum, Dept. of Prints and Drawings, 1868,0808.4320, *John Wilkes Esqr. & Liberty. Wilkes, and Liberty. A New Song* (1763); 1873,0809.1475, *English Liberty Established, Or a Mirrour for Posterity: John Wilkes* (1768).

[32] E. Vallance, 'Reborn John? The eighteenth-century afterlife of John Lilburne', *Hist. Workshop Jour.*, lxxiv (2012), 1–26, at p. 16.

[33] Vallance, 'Reborn John?', p. 16.

[34] Breay and Harrison, *Magna Carta: Law, Liberty, Legacy*, pp. 170–3.

[35] G. A. Godden, *Illustrated Encyclopaedia of British Pottery and Porcelain* (1966), p. 146; Victoria & Albert Museum, 414:1109/&A-1885, 'John Wilkes Teapot', Wedgwood, *c*.1770; Brighton Museum, DA328528, Thomas Radford, 'John Wilkes Teapot', Derby, *c*.1770.

Beardmore (d. 1771) an attorney and editor of a whig journal *The Monitor*.[36] Closely associated with Wilkes, Beardmore had led a sustained campaign against the earl of Bute's ministry – in particular over the issues of General Warrants and illegal detention, the closeness of Bute to the king, and the tyranny of the Stamp Act (1712) which raised the price of newspapers beyond the pocket of the average reader.

Reasonably cheap, uncensored and scurrilous, newspapers proved an effective way of cultivating public hostility towards the tyranny of the government and it is no surprise that both Wilkes and Beardmore used them as their main medium of criticism.[37] The king's ministers responded using all legal means they could to dampen and terminate any critical publications. Arresting the printers and authors wholesale was the most effective method and this was often undertaken by the use of General Warrants, which – contrary to Magna Carta – were issued to arrest any person suspected of involvement in a publication and authorized the searching of their property until evidence of criminal activity was found.[38] Liberty of expression and argument was regarded as fundamental to a legitimate political polity and the 'birth-right of a Briton' as the 'firmest bulwark of the liberties of this country'; yet, General Warrants, Beardmore and Wilkes argued, threatened these rights by undermining the freedom of the individual and the freedom of the press to criticize illegitimate government.[39] For publicizing such views Beardmore was arrested under a General Warrant in 1762 (followed closely by Wilkes in 1763).[40]

Upon his arrest Beardmore ensured that he was apprehended in his study while in the act of teaching his son Magna Carta.[41] This tableau became the subject of a much reproduced painting by the radical portraitist Robert Edge Pine (1730–88) who would go on to paint Wilkes and whose own father, John Pine (1690–1756), had earlier reproduced the first detailed engraving of the Great Charter in 1733.[42] Veneration of Magna Carta clearly ran in the family. Duplicated as a print by James Watson (1740–90) this popular image depicts Beardmore in fine cloak and wig pointing out

---

[36] A. H. Cash, *John Wilkes: the Scandalous Father of Civil Liberty* (2006), pp. 88–9.

[37] See B. Harris, *Politics and the Rise of the Press: Britain and France, 1620–1800* (1996), pp. 29–52.

[38] H. Barker, *Newspapers, Politics and English Society, 1695–1855* (Harlow, 2000), p. 71.

[39] *The North Briton*, no. 1, 5 Jun. 1762, in J. Wilkes, *The North Briton from No. 1 to No. XLVI. Inclusive. With Several Useful and Explanatory Notes not Printed in any Former Edition* (1769), p. 1.

[40] Thomas, *John Wilkes: a Friend to Liberty*, pp. 23, 27–30. Interestingly, upon Wilkes's arrest Beardmore acted as his solicitor.

[41] Pallister, *Magna Carta: the Heritage of Liberty*, p. 60, n. 3.

[42] Breay and Harrison, *Magna Carta: Law, Liberty, Legacy*, pp. 216–217.

chapter 29 of the 1225 charter stating in Latin, 'Nullus liber homo cap[iatur] vel imprisionetur aut' ('No freeman shall be arrested or imprisoned …'); listening intently his young son absorbs the principles of liberty.[43] To emphasize the constitutional iconography of the print the inscription below notes Beardmore is a 'Common Council-man of the City of London' and quoting Deuteronomy explicitly connects Magna Carta's sacred (almost religious) political principles of freedom with Beardmore's act of resistance. The print was immensely popular, inspiring parodies such as that depicting the infamous eighteenth-century criminal 'Dick Swift' teaching his son an altered version of the ten commandments with the print of Beardmore pinned to the back wall.[44]

From such Wilkite prints contemporaries in Britain and the North American colonies – who by the late 1760s were beginning to agitate against what they considered to be a tyrannical British government – learnt how powerful the Great Charter was as a symbol of liberty for their own propaganda and at times conflated issues based around their invocation of Magna Carta.[45] In 1768 in the lead up to the American War of Independence the Massachusetts house of representatives commissioned the famous Liberty Bowl which, with Magna Carta emblazoned on it, celebrated both John Wilkes as an opponent of the king and the 'Glorious Ninety-Two' American politicians who challenged British laws imposing heavy taxation on the American colonies.[46] Helped by Beardmore and Wilkes the 1760s saw a strong revival of the tradition of Magna Carta as a powerful public resource, a symbol readily mobilized and contested by political factions. Its regular adornment on popular prints, porcelain and in the press ensured that the prominence of the Great Charter in the legal textbooks was translated into a shared cultural appreciation. Certainly, this was part of a process that was begun in the seventeenth century but with industrialization in the eighteenth and nineteenth centuries the rate and range of its appearance and dissemination was rapidly accelerated.

Unsurprisingly, during a period dominated by agitation for parliamentary reform and challenges to the repressive measures implemented by the British government following the American and French revolutions, the

---

[43] Brit. Museum, Dept. of Prints and Drawings, 1902,1011.6373, J. Watson, *Arthur Beardmore, Common Council-man of the City of London, Teaching his Son Magna Charta* (1765). See also Breay and Harrison, *Magna Carta: Law, Liberty, Legacy*, p. 174.

[44] Brit. Museum, Dept. of Prints and Drawings, 1851,0308.607, *Dick Swift Thieftaker of the City of London Teaching his Son the Commandments* (1765). See also Breay and Harrison, *Magna Carta: Law, Liberty, Legacy*, p. 175.

[45] A. Lock, 'Magna Carta: the Atlantic crossing', *History Today*, lxv (2015), 31–7, at pp. 36–7.

[46] Boston, Museum of Fine Arts, Acc. no. 49.45, P. Revere, Jr., Sons of Liberty Bowl, 1768.

instances in which the liberties of Magna Carta were depicted proliferated. Its appearance in the print media and in major political trials of radicals was pervasive. It was exploited by both supporters and opponents of Charles James Fox (1749–1806) during the Regency Crisis of 1788; invoked on tokens disseminated by members of the London Corresponding Society celebrating their acquittal at their trials in 1794; used to challenge the suspension of habeas corpus in 1817; and raised during the Queen Caroline affair of 1820.[47] Of all these early nineteenth-century invocations, however, it was perhaps most audaciously used in court by the Cato Street conspirators at their trials for high treason in 1820. These Spencean radicals had conspired to assassinate the entire British cabinet at a banquet but were arrested in their hideout having been betrayed by an agent provocateur.[48] For one of the conspirators, William Davidson (1786–1820), the plot to murder the cabinet was perfectly justified by Magna Carta.[49] He likened himself and his co-conspirators to the twenty-five barons nominated in clause 61 to uphold the Great Charter should the government tyrannically ignore its provisions. Describing clause 61, Davidson argued that the Great Charter,

> ordained that twenty-five barons should be nominated to see that the terms of the charter were not infringed; and, if it was found that his Majesty's Ministers were guilty of such infringement, then four barons were to call upon them for redress. If this were not granted, then the four barons were to return to their brethren … to take up arms, and assert their rights. Such an act was not considered in times of old as an act of treason towards the king, however hostile it might be towards his ministers.[50]

Needless to say this highly inaccurate interpretation of clause 61 did not persuade the judge and Davidson was sentenced with six of his other co-conspirators to be hanged, drawn and quartered: the last time this sentence was passed at the Old Bailey.[51]

---

[47] Brit. Museum, Dept. of Prints and Drawings, 1952,0403.3, 'Design for a column with a statue of William III, intended to be erected at Runnymede, 1788; 1868,0808.5828, *Revolution Pillar* (1788); 1868,0808.8364, G. Cruikshank, *Liberty Suspended* (1817); Manchester, People's History Museum, 1993.371–94, 'Erskine and Gibbs and Trial by Jury', token, 1794; Hone and Cruikshank, *The Queen and Magna Charta*. See also Breay and Harrison, *Magna Carta: Law, Liberty, Legacy*, pp. 176–7, 181.

[48] M. Chase, 'Cato Street conspirators', in *Oxford Dictionary of National Biography* (Oxford, 2004–15) <https://doi.org/10.1093/ref:odnb/58584> [accessed 26 March 2018].

[49] For more on William Davidson, see H. Mackey, 'The complexion of the accused: William Davidson, the black revolutionary in the Cato Street conspiracy', *Negro Educational Rev.*, xxiii (1972), 132–47.

[50] G. T. Wilkinson, *An Authentic History of the Cato Street Conspiracy* (1820), p. 341.

[51] C. Emsley, T. Hitchcock and R. Shoemaker, 'Punishments at the Old Bailey: drawn

While it was invoked predominantly by those challenging the government and seeking parliamentary reform, many loyalist prints also engaged Magna Carta throughout the period to contest what they perceived to be the dangerous Jacobin propaganda of the reformers. Presenting Magna Carta as the basis of an authentic ancient liberty, these loyalists argued that the Great Charter was being undermined by British radicals eager to replicate the excesses of French republicanism, which – when 'contrasted' with England's unwritten 'ancient constitution' – offered nothing but misery, poverty and slavery. This argument was made in *The Palace of John Bull, Contrasted with the Poor "House that Jack Built"* (1820) whose title page displayed 'the fair SCALES of JUSTICE' weighing up the radicals' Phrygian cap and quill against the Habeas Corpus Act, the Bill of Rights and Magna Carta. While the scales were weighed down with the substance of these weighty 'Laws of renown', the radicals' republican ideals were unsurprisingly found to be hollow and wanting.[52] An earlier print of 1792 by Thomas Rowlandson (1757–1827) entitled *The Contrast*, similarly asserted this popular loyalist point. First printed in the aftermath of the September Massacres and the arrest of Louis XVI, the print employed the familiar iconography of 'British Liberty' – represented in this case by Britannia holding the scales of justice and Magna Carta – to undermine radical arguments about the benefits of republicanism and 'French Liberty' which were represented in the print by an ugly, blood-stained, Medusa-like Marianne.[53]

Although invoked by both loyalist and radical alike, engagement with Magna Carta remained unsubtle and unsophisticated in the late eighteenth and early nineteenth centuries and largely copied the iconographical tropes already established by the likes of Wilkes and Beardmore in the 1760s. The most obvious example of this can be seen in the exploitation of Magna Carta by the radical M.P. Sir Francis Burdett (1770–1844) who was committed to the Tower of London in 1810 on the orders of the house of commons for breach of parliamentary privilege having publicly criticized, in a deliberately provocative open letter to his constituents, another prosecution by the commons of the London-based radical John Gale Jones (1769–1838).[54]

---

and quartered', in *Old Bailey Proceedings Online* <http://www.oldbaileyonline.org/static/Punishment.jsp#death> [accessed 27 Sept. 2017].

[52] *The Palace of John Bull, Contrasted with the Poor "House that Jack Built"* (1820).

[53] Brit. Museum, Dept. of Prints and Drawings, 1861,1012.47, T. Rowlandson, *The Contrast: British Liberty, French Liberty, Which is Best?* (1792); Breay and Harrison, *Magna Carta: Law, Liberty, Legacy*, p. 158.

[54] Pallister, *Magna Carta: the Heritage of Liberty*, pp. 67–9. Gale Jones had been imprisoned for publicly questioning the legitimacy of parliament to exclude strangers from the house of commons during its debates of the failed Walcheren expedition.

Throughout his career Burdett was a staunch advocate of radical parliamentary reform with a deep and long held attachment to the Cokean interpretation of the existence of an 'ancient constitution' underpinned by Magna Carta.[55] For Burdett, Magna Carta represented a powerful emblem of the 'ancient' freedoms and 'birthright of Britons' that had been long lost through the misrule of a corrupt political establishment in need of reform.[56] Upon his imprisonment in 1810 Burdett drew extensively on these ideas appealing to the Great Charter with enormous popular success. Indeed, the published open letter to his constituents for which he was imprisoned eulogized the Charter throughout and opened with Magna Carta's clauses 39 and 40 as its epigraph.[57] Published in William Cobbett's *Political Register* Burdett's letter continued the debate of a century earlier regarding the sovereignty of an unrepresentative parliament. He informed his constituents that the Commons' vote imprisoning Gale Jones amounted 'to a declaration, that an Order of theirs is to be of more weight than Magna Charta and the Laws of the Land'; as such, Burdett questioned 'Whether our liberty be still ... secured by the laws of our forefathers, or ... at the absolute mercy of a part of our fellow-subjects, collected together by means which it is not necessary for me to describe'.[58] The corollary of the argument was that a reformed parliament, elected on a wide franchise, would not dare to so infringe the rights of their subjects and, as they represented the people, could not but abide by the 'ancient constitution' as its guardians.

This interpretation of the arbitrary and unconstitutional actions of the house of commons against Gale Jones and Burdett gained traction. Throughout his imprisonment colourful prints and porcelain – reminiscent of Wilkes – proliferated depicting Burdett as the champion of Magna Carta and British liberty and, following Beardmore before him, Burdett even arranged to be arrested at home teaching his son Magna Carta while a growing mob outside caused a disturbance.[59] According to M. Dorothy George, hardly ever before had a public character been so hero-worshipped

[55] M. Baer, 'Burdett, Sir Francis, fifth baronet (1770–1844)', in *O.D.N.B.* <https://doi.org/10.1093/ref:odnb/3962> [accessed 26 March 2018]..

[56] Turner, *Magna Carta through the Ages*, p. 185; *The London Magazine and Review, January to April 1825*, new ser., i (1825), 518.

[57] F. Burdett, *Sir Francis Burdett to his Constituents; Denying the Power of the House of Commons to Imprison the People of England* (1810), pp. 3–12. The letter was first published in William Cobbett's *Political Register*, xvii (1810), *Sir Francis Burdett to his Constituents*, cols. 417–22.

[58] Burdett, *Sir Francis Burdett to his Constituents*, p. 5.

[59] Brit. Museum., Dept. of Prints and Drawings, 1868,1212.1, I. Cruikshank, *The Arrest of Sir Fs Burdett. MP* (1810); R. K. Huch, *The Radical Lord Radnor: the Public Life of Viscount Folkestone, Third Earl of Radnor (1779–1869)* (Minneapolis, Minn., 1977), p. 65.

or glamorized in satirical prints.[60] Burdett represented an attack on 'corruption' in all its facets and recalling Wilkes and Beardmore, the Charter was the centrepiece in a symbolic performance calculated to mobilize public opinion against the government and the sovereignty of an unrepresentative parliament.[61]

Such powerful radical propaganda created a strong connection between Magna Carta and parliamentary reform in the popular imagination. Indeed, so strong was it that when the Reform Act of 1832 was passed, granting new political rights in the form of a limited extension of the franchise, it was explicitly presented as a new Magna Carta. Early published editions of the Act were issued under the title of *The Great Charter of 1832* while a popular ceramic cordial bottle representing the lord chancellor, Henry Brougham (1778–1868) – who played a crucial role in the passage of the Bill through the house of lords – identified the Act as 'The Second Magna Charta'.[62] Other M.P.s involved in passing the legislation similarly relished the comparison. The M.P. Thomas Coke (1754–1842), a descendent of the seventeenth-century lawyer Sir Edward Coke, commissioned a relief celebrating the Reform Act depicting him with his whig parliamentary colleagues forcing King John to seal the Charter at Runnymede.[63]

This was not the last time that Magna Carta would be raised in connection with parliamentary reform in the nineteenth century. The Great Reform Act of 1832 was but the first in a series of legislative developments that paved the way to universal suffrage in Great Britain in 1928 and in the agitation for these later reforms Magna Carta continued to be lionized. Most prominent in this respect, however, was its use by the Chartists between 1838 and the early 1850s. The first mass working-class movement for democratic rights, Chartism took its name from the *People's Charter* that contained the six points of parliamentary reform for which they agitated.[64] The choice of the word 'charter' in this context was significant. It consciously drew upon the powerful symbolism of Magna Carta as the foundation stone of English liberties. The allusion to Magna Carta was one which all politically engaged

---

[60] George, *English Political Caricature 1793–1832*, ii. 125.

[61] George, *English Political Caricature 1793–1832*, ii. 125–7. See also Breay and Harrison, *Magna Carta: Law, Liberty, Legacy*, pp. 178–80.

[62] *The Great Charter of 1832; Comprised in the Three Reform Bills* (1832); People's History Museum, NMLH.1992.1073, 'Ceramic cordial bottle with Lord Brougham and a Second Magna Charta', Doulton & Watts, 1832.

[63] N. B. Penny, 'The whig cult of Fox in early nineteenth-century sculpture', *Past & Present*, lxx (1976), 94–105, at p. 104. The relief can still be seen at the Coke family seat at Holkham Hall, Norfolk.

[64] D. Thompson, 'Chartism, success or failure?', in *People for the People: Radical Ideas and Personalities in British History*, ed. D. Rubinstein (1973), pp. 90–7, at p. 92.

contemporaries would have been aware. It continued the long tradition of radical appropriation of the Great Charter and in so doing represented the *People's Charter* as a new Magna Carta that would ultimately secure the political rights of all classes, completing the process begun in 1215.[65] Yet, again, as with Wilkes or Burdett, the Chartist's invocation of Magna Carta was made without any serious reference to its actual historical contexts. It was largely used in an anachronistic way to claim rights that were never guaranteed in the Charter and that were quite unknown to the medieval mind.

For all these inaccuracies, however, Magna Carta remained a powerful totem celebrated by the crowd. At a great Chartist meeting on Hartshead Moor, near Leeds, in 1838 the demagogue Joseph Rayner Stephens (1805–79) addressed those gathered, inaccurately invoking Magna Carta as ensuring free speech, freedom of association and even freedom from the workhouse; he told them,

> We are seeking nothing new … We stand upon our old rights – we seek no change – we say give us the good old laws of England unchanged (Cheers.) … and what are those laws? What is that constitution by which we seek to abide? – (Magna Charta) – Aye, Magna Charta! The good old laws of English freedom – free meetings – freedom of speech – freedom of workshops – freedom of homesteads – free and happy firesides, and no workhouses. (Cheers)[66]

A year later when Stephens was imprisoned for disturbing the public peace the Manchester Chartist R. J. Richardson (1808?–1861) threatened to march into the city with 100,000 men holding copies of Magna Carta in their hands.[67]

The Chartists were by no means the last political movement to invoke Magna Carta in the long nineteenth century which saw the Charter persist as a useful symbol of legitimate political rights. Led by the eccentric lawyer Dr. Edward Kenealy (1819–80), the Magna Charta Association established in 1874 promoted a broad reformist agenda that built upon the earlier demands of the Chartists. Receiving widespread national support, it became, according to Rohan McWilliam, 'the most significant movement of popular agitation between the decline of Chartism in the 1840s and rise of organised socialism in the 1880s'.[68] The suffragettes of the late nineteenth and early

---

[65] M. Chase, *Chartism: a New History* (Manchester, 2007), p. 8. This argument was most powerfully put in the Chartist pamphlet J. Watkins, *The Five Cardinal Points of the People's Charter* (Whitby, 1839), pp. 4–6.

[66] *Northern Star*, 16 Oct. 1838, p. 2.

[67] Taylor, 'Magna Carta in the nineteenth century', p. 147.

[68] J. A. Hamilton and R. McWilliam, 'Kenealy, Edward Vaughan Hyde (1819–1880)', in *O.D.N.B.* <https://doi.org/10.1093/ref:odnb/15356> [accessed 26 March 2018];

twentieth centuries also used Magna Carta in their own propaganda to legitimize direct political action. In 1911 the suffragette newspaper *Votes for Women* drew on the example of the Magna Carta barons and 'How Militant Methods Won the Great Charter' to encourage their readers to continue in their shock tactics.[69] Others such as the first practising female barrister Helena Normanton (1882–1957) engaged with Magna Carta as a historical precedent that supported the right of women to vote. For Normanton,

> it is expressly contrary to Magna Carta to refuse, deny, *or delay*, right or justice. The right of franchise is still unconstitutionally withheld from women, but the spirit of Magna Carta sounds a trumpet-call to them to struggle ever more valiantly to realise its noble ideal.[70]

Ironically, these later appeals to Magna Carta were made at almost precisely the same time that the clauses of the Great Charter were being repealed by parliament. Beginning in 1828 and concluding in 1969 the biggest excision of Magna Carta's clauses from the Statute took place in 1863 as part of the Statute Law Revision Act (26 & 27 Vic. c.125).[71] Today only three clauses remain in English law.[72] However, the fact that Magna Carta was losing its basis in law seemed to matter very little to those who invoked it. From the early eighteenth century the Charter had been engaged with less as a legal instrument than as a versatile and powerful totem of an ancient English liberty. It lent the semblance of political legitimacy to anyone who wished to capitalize upon it and its ability to stir emotional public support has ensured its legacy as a powerful international symbol of freedom up to the present day.

R. McWilliam, 'Radicalism and popular culture: the Tichborne case and the politics of "fair play" 1867–1886', in *Currents of Radicalism: Popular Radicalism, Organised Labour and Party Politics in Britain 1850–1914*, ed. E. F. Biagini and A. J. Reid (Cambridge, 1991), pp. 44–64, at p. 44.

[69] *Votes for Women*, 27 Jan. 1911. See also Taylor, 'Magna Carta in the nineteenth century', pp. 149–50.

[70] H. Normanton, 'Magna Carta and Women', *The Englishwomen*, lxxvii (1915), 129–42, at p. 135.

[71] Breay and Harrison, *Magna Carta: Law, Liberty, Legacy*, p. 221.

[72] Vincent, *Magna Carta: a Very Short Introduction*, pp. 101–2. The clauses still on Statute all date from the reissue of Magna Carta confirmed by Edward I and enrolled on the Statute in 1297. They are: clause 1 confirming the liberties of the English Church; clause 9 confirming the liberties and customs of the city of London and other cities, towns and ports; and, the most famous, clause 29 stating that 'No freeman will be taken or imprisoned or disseised or outlawed or exiled or in anyway ruined … save by the lawful judgement of his peers or by the law of the land. To no one shall we sell, to no one shall we deny or delay right or justice'.

Index

INSTITUTE OF HISTORICAL RESEARCH | SCHOOL OF ADVANCED STUDY UNIVERSITY OF LONDON

The Institute of Historical Research (I.H.R.) is the U.K.'s national centre for history. Founded in 1921, the Institute facilitates and promotes innovative research via its primary collections library, and its programme of training, publishing, conferences, seminars and fellowships. The I.H.R. is one of the nine humanities research institutes of the School of Advanced Study at the University of London.

'I.H.R. Shorts' is a new Open Access publishing series from the Institute of Historical Research at the University of London. Insightful and concise, I.H.R. Shorts offer incisive commentaries on contemporary historical debates. Titles range from 15,000 to 50,000 words with a focus on interdisciplinary approaches to the past.

1. Dethroning historical reputations: universities, museums and the commemoration of benefactors
   edited by Jill Pellew and Lawrence Goldman (2018)

2. Magna Carta: history, context and influence
   edited by Lawrence Goldman (2018)

CPSIA information can be obtained
at www.ICGtesting.com
Printed in the USA
JSHW022226211219
3115JS00001B/9